Wilson Stuart

English philosophical Styles

Six Studies

Wilson Stuart

English philosophical Styles
Six Studies

ISBN/EAN: 9783337070878

Printed in Europe, USA, Canada, Australia, Japan

Cover: Foto ©ninafisch / pixelio.de

More available books at **www.hansebooks.com**

The Victoria University.

1899.

ENGLISH PHILOSOPHICAL STYLES;

(SIX STUDIES.)

An Essay for which the John Bright Scholarship was awarded in 1897.

BY

WILSON STUART,
M.A. & B.Sc. (VICT.).

Philosophia simulari potest, eloquentia non potest. (QUINCT.)

MANCHESTER:
J. E. CORNISH, 16, ST. ANN'S SQUARE.
1899.

CONTENTS.

	PAGE
NOTE ...	4
I. FRANCIS BACON (1560—1626)	5
II. THOMAS HOBBES (1588—1679)	... 24
III. JOHN LOCKE (1632—1704)	... 40
IV. GEORGE BERKELEY (1685—1753) ...	... 57
V. DAVID HUME (1711—1776)	... 73
VI. JOHN STUART MILL (1806—1873)	... 90

NOTE.

THE John Bright Scholarship was founded (mainly out of the surplus of the subscriptions to the Rochdale statue of the late Mr. Bright) for the encouragement of the study of English Literature in the Victoria University. It is awarded biennially for a book or essay on some subject directly connected with the study of English Literature, and its value is £100. The candidates must be persons who have obtained the Degree of B.A. in the University, and have not completed more than two years from the date of the examination qualifying them for the B.A. Degree. They must also have attended at least one year's full course of lectures on English Literature in a College of the University. A number of alternative subjects are set for candidates to select from. The other conditions of the Scholarship can be seen in the Victoria University *Calendar* (1899, p. 172).

The Scholarship in 1897 was awarded to an Essay by the present writer on "English Philosophical Styles," and the Essay was recommended by the Adjudicators to the University for publication. The substance of it appears here under the original title, restricted by the phrase, "Six Studies." The writer found it impossible to exhaust the subject included under the original comprehensive title. It was thought better, therefore, to select so many of the names in English Philosophical literature as could be dealt with in the form of studies within a space about equal to that filled by the Prize Essay. This has meant omitting several writers of great importance—Butler, Hamilton, Mr. Herbert Spencer—who were considered at some length in the original Essay; and remarks on minor writers have been excluded. The need of the Introduction, which was taken up largely with a consideration of the scope of the subject, has been obviated by limiting the title. Some recasting has been necessary, in order to adapt the writing to the form of independent sections; but the original lent itself to this treatment. The extracts are almost entirely the same, and much of the composition is as it was.

I.

Francis Bacon.

LORD BACON was one of the leading actors in English History, and one of the greatest masters of the English tongue. He is known as the father of modern thought ; he is certainly the father of modern philosophical literature, for he is the first great writer of philosophy in the modern spirit and in a modern language.[1] Before the time of Bacon, English civilization had not been of the sort to produce an indigenous philosophy. Though during the Middle Ages there had been multitudes of students in the Universities of Europe saturating themselves with the old Aristotelian doctrines, a more barren time for producing philosophical literature and native systems of thought cannot be imagined. Men seemed to await a Bacon who could sweep aside the methods of antiquity, and declare a new era to have opened for the human race. To appreciate the gigantic intellect that put itself athwart the world's thought and knowledge has proved one of the absorbing tasks of that posterity to whom Lord Bacon bequeathed his name and fame. To judge the character and to estimate the philosophy of Bacon are two of the knottiest problems of biography and of the history of thought respectively. But the true secret of his greatness lies neither in his moral character nor in the particular ideas that he evolved, but rather in his spirit and in his style. And the inspiration is in the style, because that is the very countenance and expression of the great spirit within. " He had that mysterious gift to which M. " Charles de Rémusat assigns the first place among the causes of his " influence in the world—the quality which he calls *greatness,* and " supposes to reside rather in the manner than in the thought."[2] Bacon

---
[1] Descartes did not publish his *Discours de la Méthode* until 1637, while Bacon's *Advancement of Learning* is dated 1605, and the *Novum Organum* 1620.
[2] Ellis and Spedding's Ed. of Bacon's Works, Vol. VII. (Life), pp. 574-5.

did not elaborate a system, he formulated a method. The conception of that method was the work of genius, but its theoretical and practical worth does not explain Bacon's unparalleled influence over the modern world. No doubt, ideas were all-essential, but how comparatively few and simple were the instruments of his achievements! Bacon's formulas have become curiosities, but the spirit that animated his whole enterprise has rendered his work immortal. As it has been well put, "Though this [Method], the favourite child of Bacon's genius "which he would fain have made heir of all he had, died thus in the "cradle, his genius itself still lives and works among us."[1] It is not so much Bacon's philosophy as his philosophical style—using that term in its broadest sense—that is the secret of his power. It is the pervading influence of a majestic yet simple and earnest spirit that has made his writings one of the most powerful inspirations of the modern world, its science and its letters. Bacon's work was the result of marvellous confidence in, and reliance upon the powers of man, combined with a becoming humility in the presence of nature's forces and nature's secrets. The confidence and humility, dignity and reverence, that formed the unique spirit of Bacon were of such a character that in him each attained the very acme of its own perfection. It is impossible to say that either was the more essential quality for his work. Few human beings can have been endowed with more confidence and buoyant hope than Bacon; yet his message to the world was, that the secret for the attainment of true knowledge is humility of spirit.

Scholasticism may be said to have failed through an overweening confidence in the capacity of man's unaided intellect and by the want of self-abnegation in the approach to nature. Man had attained to civilization and to arts; he had organized societies, instituted laws and erected systems of knowledge all after his own ideas. And as life became artificial, man to some extent forgot that he was *of* nature, and treated with careless indifference the teachings of Nature herself. This could not be among those children of nature, the Greeks; but in the Middle Ages it was the curse that produced barrenness. But after centuries of man's legislating for nature and evolving out of the recesses of his own reason systems to determine what it was fit for Nature to be and to perform, the force of facts began to bear it in upon men's minds that Nature goes her own way and that the facts of existence are not

---

[1] *Ibid.*, Vol. III., p. 171.

to be anticipated by the ideas of man. There began to dawn here and there the scientific consciousness; men endowed with the instinct of science learned the lesson of humility of spirit in the presence of Nature: patient investigators like Galileo, Harvey, and Gilbert made themselves her willing slaves and, in turn, were entrusted with her secrets. But these men, though born discoverers and possessed of ingenious minds, were not fitted to head a great intellectual movement. Their work was to some extent secret, ashamed of itself, overshadowed and cowed by enthroned systems. They had not that breadth of intellectual vision, that splendid, daring confidence which was necessary for the formulation of new methods of knowledge and for the inauguration of a new scientific era. Their investigations were carried out in deep humility, but they themselves lacked the greatness of spirit necessary for the vindication of their calling against the appearance of pettiness and servility. No doubt the physical researches of such men indicated an intellectual awakening that could not brook the bondage of false systems however august; but particular contradictions of the dogmatic assertions of antiquity could not be appreciated in their full import by the mass of men. Nay, the full meaning of the discoveries and of the methods by which they were made, was not apprehended by the discoverers themselves: they worked instinctively. There had, indeed, from time to time appeared men with a broader and more philosophic cast of mind than the ordinary physical investigator, who had rebelled against the tyranny of an antiquated system. But their influence was comparatively feeble; the times were not ready; and they were so far from revolutionizing the world's thought that they themselves were broken against the stubborn, solid wall of Scholasticism. Bruno and Campanella were such. The effete, archaic mass of Scholastic dogma, though secretly undermined by the modern spirit, was still bolstered up by the tradition, authority, and prestige of the learned and the powerful in Church and State. No feeble weapons of the diffident, cramped specialist could avail. What was needed at this juncture was an intellect of sufficient magnitude and grasp to generalise into principles the new way of knowledge, a man with the inspiration and enthusiasm that comes from realising the unbounded possibilities of human knowledge and of human progress; there was needed the boldness, the ambition, the undaunted hope and courage of a great leader of men, organiser of enterprise, director of new energies, commander of new movements; there must be the dignity and confidence of one, who with lordly pomp and imperiousness of manner could sweep aside a massive and formerly influential system as obsolete, and who, by his whole-hearted support, could strengthen the efforts of humble investigators. Bacon was the man and the only man who, by his greatness of spirit, compass of thought, instinctive appreciation of the new movement, command of language in which to express the new ideas, impressiveness of rhetoric, magnificence of manner, and unique position for gaining an audience both in England and on the Continent, was fitted to represent the greatness of the new Kingdom of Man over nature, and to command, by words that could not be ignored, the attention of the world at large to the revolution of thought that was taking place.

Bacon's mature plan for his philosophical exposition was to compose his works as the several parts of an *Instauratio Magna*. The dimensions of the work and the spirit in which it was undertaken are indicated in the *Prefatio* and the *Distributio Operis*, which were prefixed to the *Novum Organum*. The *Instauratio* is to be divided into six parts. These may be described briefly in the words of Mr. Ellis. "The first is to contain a general survey of the present state of "knowledge. In the second men are to be taught how to use their "understanding aright in the investigation of Nature. In the third all "the phenomena of the universe are to be stored up as in a treasure-"house, as the materials on which the new method is to be employed. "In the fourth examples are to be given of its operation and of the "results to which it leads. The fifth is to contain what Bacon had "accomplished in natural philosophy without the aid of his own "method . . . It is therefore less important than the rest, . . . "Moreover its value will altogether cease when the sixth part can be "completed, wherein will be set forth the new philosophy—the result of "the application of the new method to all the phenomena of the universe. "But to complete this, the last part of the Instauratio, Bacon does not "hope; he speaks of it as a thing 'et supra vires et ultra spes nostras "collocata.'"[1] Indeed, of these six parts only the first two attained to anything like completion. The instalments that came out under Part Three deal with the natural history of phenomena and are unimportant for Bacon's general philosophy. The formal members of the *Instauratio* are in Latin: Part I. being represented by the *De Augmentis Scientiarum* and Part II. by the *Novum Organum*.

---

[1] R. L. Ellis, Preface to *Novum Organum*, Bacon's Works, Vol. I., p. 71.

Since Bacon broke so completely with the past in aim and spirit, we are surprised that he should have taken to the old Latin language to express himself; and as all his ideas bear the stamp of the new age, it is remarkable that he should have succeeded in making them current in an antiquated tongue. If Bacon had been a Scholastic we could have understood his preference for Latin, but there must be some very weighty reason to account for the fact that the man, whose position is due to his innovations, chooses to connect himself with that vain mediæval philosophy by employing its language, when he might have completed the severance by using English solely.

There appear to have been two reasons for this clinging to antiquity in the matter of language. First and foremost, he was confident that his was a great work, not for one generation or one nation merely, but a work that would revolutionize the world's thought and discoveries: he must therefore have a world's language in which to deposit it. He had no confidence (and he tells us so), in English as being stable enough to be entrusted with what he regards as the world's future handbook of rules and principles for science and philosophy. The fact is that he had infinitely more confidence in his own philosophy than in the English language as its vehicle. English was good enough for most books that had hitherto been written in it; the drama and ephemeral polemics might be entrusted to it; but for a great system of philosophy he regarded it with suspicion, as untrustworthy and untried. Moreover, English appealed to comparatively few philosophers and scientists. Bacon, therefore, chose the universal language of science and law to proclaim universal knowledge and promulgate "a great piece of philosophical legislation."

Secondly, there is such elevation, grandeur, dignity, and lordly breadth in his conception that Bacon instinctively used Latin for his most completed expression. The state and pomp of Latin is suggested as natural by the very roll of his sentences and the grandeur of his thought. Still, in its native purity, Latin is unsuited to philosophical abstractions and metaphysical subtlety. The success which Bacon achieved is due to the fact that the Latin he uses is Scholastic in vocabulary and construction, and retains his own characteristic English style. The genius of the Latin tongue was for the concrete, not the abstract. Its avoidance of even simple abstractions made it especially inappropriate for Bacon, who gained great clearness and emphasis by the constant use of abstract substantives, with genitives following, in preference to qualifying adjectives. The annexed will illustrate this style:—

"... the largeness of your capacity, the faithfulness of your memory, the swiftness of your apprehension, the penetration of your judgment, and the facility and order of your elocution."[1]

"The derogations therefore which grow to learning from the fortune or condition of learned men, are either in respect of scarcity of means, or in respect of privateness of life and meanness of employment."[2]

Greek philosophical writing was often ambiguous and inexact prior to Aristotle's invention of an abstract terminology, which, however, he accomplished only by doing violence to the genius of the Greek language, just as Latin was inadequate until Scholasticism improved and at the same time spoiled it. Plato often struggles in vain to portray, by his ingenuity and imaginative power, his views on his own "Theory of Ideas," while Aristotle was able to put the case exactly by the invention of the technical abstract terms of Logic. Bacon did not realize the inadequacy and unsuitableness of Latin for the new thoughts and spirit. For its elasticity, directness, and naturalness, he instinctively wrote in English; for its universal currency, its dignity, and stability he translated into Latin; but that language was only persuaded to tell his message by much coaxing and ingenuity.

Owing to Bacon's careful and laborious way of compiling his works—re-casting, re-writing, and translating—they have become considerably complicated, and it is not easy to decide what are to be regarded as examples of his English philosophical style. His chief works are: The *Advancement of Learning*, the *Augmentis Scientiarum*, and the *Novum Organum*. The *Essays* are not, in strict sense, philosophical. They contain many practical moral maxims and much worldly prudence, but not his systematic thought. The *New Atlantis* sets forth a Utopia in the form of a philosophical tale; but though entirely in sympathy with, it forms no part of Bacon's body of philosophy. The *Sylva Sylvarum, Historia Ventorum, Historia Vitæ et Mortis*, &c., have no interest for us. Several early tentative productions that were superseded by the *Novum Organum* are of no direct importance. Of Bacon's three great works, the Latin expansion of the *Advancement of Learning*, called *De Augmentis Scientiarum*, may be neglected for our

---

[1] *Advancement of Learning*, Bk. i. (Works), Vol. III., p. 261.
[2] *Ibid.*, p. 274.

purpose. The original *Advancement*, one of the earliest of Bacon's writings, is philosophical, though not in so high a degree as the *Novum Organum*. It is introductory, and shows the author's general attitude towards the question of human knowledge. It is an English masterpiece, and is an admirable example of Bacon's English prose. His method and principles are formulated in the *Novum Organum*, which is undoubtedly his greatest work, and one of the monuments of the world's philosophy. Though it has a Latin dress and title, we think it may be justly claimed as an English work with an English style. It is certainly not Latin literature; and at every stage through which the *Novum Organum* developed, the Latin representative was preceded by the same work, either in germ or in complete form, in English.[1]

There has been some controversy as to how far, if at all, Bacon was master of the art of Latin composition. Liebig has asserted, but wrongly, that Bacon himself wrote none of his works in Latin, and that he got his friends to translate his English writings. Bacon did,

---

[1] The *Novum Organum* was the result of careful elaboration and many preliminary efforts. It received revision every year for twelve years. Its germ is to be found in the *Valerius Terminus, Of the Interpretation of Nature*, a fragment written in English probably about 1603. This was Bacon's earliest connected account of his opinions. There were several other efforts, in very distinctive styles, written apparently for experiments as to what form was suited to the subject and acceptable to the public: for Bacon was extremely concerned about the success of his work. One of the abandoned styles is exhibited in the *Temporis Partus Masculus* (Latin, about 1583). The English *Valerius Terminus* was developed into the *Partis Secundae Delineatio et Argumentum* (Latin, about 1606-7). Bacon then hit upon the plan of dealing with the subject in two parts; one an introductory work laying down principles, the other giving examples of the actual operation of the method. The first part he dealt with in his *Filum Labyrinthi sive Formula Inquisitionis* (1607), an English work. For the second part he began to draw up tables. He then translated the *Filum Labyrinthi* into Latin with only very slight alterations, and gave it the title *Cogitata et Visa* (1607). The second part he formed into a Latin piece with the title *Filum Labyrinthi, sive Inquisitio Legitima de Motu* (1607). It only remained to adapt these to the form of aphorism, and to take "heat" instead of "motion" as the example, and we have the First and Second Books respectively of the *Novum Organum*.

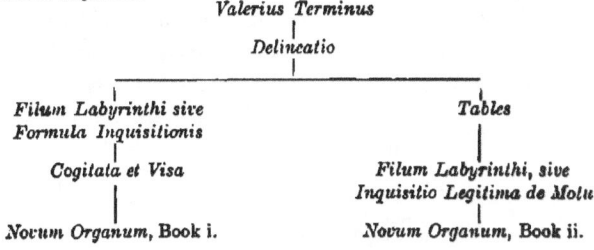

no doubt, sometimes get his English books done up in a Latin dress. But he appears to have put down his thoughts in his *Commentarius Solutus* almost indifferently in Latin or English,[1] and he himself wrote the *Novum Organum* in Latin.[2] We can gather what was Bacon's ideal of a Latin prose for his purpose from Tenison's account of the negotiations with Dr. Playfer, of Cambridge, concerning the translation of the *Advancement of Learning* which Bacon had asked him to undertake. "Upon this great occasion he [Dr. Playfer] would be over-"accurate; and he sent a specimen of such superfine Latinity that the "Lord Bacon did not encourage him to labour further in the work, in "the penning of which he desired not so much neat and polite, as clear, "masculine, and apt expression."[3] This is just the ideal he had before him in writing the *Novum Organum*. "The Latin of, at least, "the First Book of the Novum Organum, rugged and unclassical, as it "often is, seems to me . . . distinctly to bear the mark of genius, "and of the same kind of genius that we find stamped on Bacon's English "expression."[4] Thus, from the fact that the *Novum Organum* is really an English book translated into Latin words (and those often not classical), and seeing that the style is Bacon's characteristic English one, we have no hesitation in considering it as a piece of English literature.

Our author has a wonderful variety of prose wherewith to treat the different aspects of human knowledge, for that is his great theme. But in the main he has two philosophical styles, differing greatly from each other, yet both typical of the man. The one is that of the *Advancement* where we have scope for fertile imagination and need of connected discourse. Here the features are sustained eloquence, glowing imagery and grand periods. In the *Novum Organum* we have apt figures and short oracular utterances, not ornate, but compressed and clinched.

The *Advancement of Learning* is remarkably free from most of the vices which mar continuous prose of the time of Elizabeth. Bacon is the first writer to get anything like the greatest possible variety out of the English language, by uniting all the excellent features already current in the various writers. His powers range from sweeping

---

[1] Fowler, Intro. to *Novum Organum*, Sec. iv.
[2] Tenison's *Baconiana*, pp. 28, 9.
[3] *Baconiana*, p. 26.
[4] Fowler, Intro. to *Novum Organum*, Intro., p. 14.

eloquence and rich imagery to exact aphorism and striking epigram. That Bacon so combined the many and varied qualities of previous prose was due to the many-sidedness of his character, the versatility of his genius, and the diverse occupations of his life. Few if any great philosophers have manifested such wide differences in the qualities of their style, perhaps because to be a great philosopher often means to have a cramped experience and narrowed tastes. Immanuel Kant is known as the philosopher of Königsberg; and he is a monotonous, inartistic and unimaginative writer, for the most part readable only by the severest application. Bacon was at once courtier, lawyer, classical scholar, and man of the world, vocations not often united in the philosopher. The man who had been Lord Chancellor of England died from a chill taken when stuffing a hen with snow as an experiment on the power of cold to prevent putrefaction. Many interests and wide experience did much to foster a good style. The fact that he was a courtier prevented him from becoming uncouth and dry, while his profession as a legal pleader was a guarantee that his matter would be well and effectively arranged, with sufficient form and ceremony in the sentences; his classical culture filled his works with ancient lore ever ready to illustrate and adorn his modern thought.

We purpose noticing the qualities of Bacon's philosophical style in respect to the following elements:—(I.) Its broad general features, (II.) Its use of figures and illustrations, (III.) The structure of its sentences.

(I.) Perhaps the preponderant feeling we experience in reading Bacon is that of massiveness. We have not heard a solo; we have been listening to a chorus. The author had one end throughout life for all his writings. His best thought and enthusiasm were concentrated on one idea,—human knowledge and its extension for the bettering man's estate. This was a rare disposition amidst the inconsistency and flippancy of the day. Compare our author's philosophical works with the undigested, encyclopædic conglomeration of materials collected in the writings of Robert Burton and Sir Thomas Browne. Whether the form be connected discourse or isolated aphorism, the whole writing is welded together into a solid unity by the intense feeling of a man who writes because an all-absorbing thought has taken possession of his entire mind. Bacon's thoughts are not pieced and joined; they are fused. A mere *littérateur*, a dealer in curiosities and fancy goods, might indeed force an elastic band round his whole stock-in-trade and label the lot, but Bacon's writings have the organic unity and the massiveness worthy of a great philosopher. As the result of such devotion to his subject there is a genuine earnestness and a simple enthusiasm of style in spite of all the dignity and grandeur of his bearing. There is a whole-heartedness that enlists our sympathies and an appeal that commands our efforts.

"And now we have spoken of the several kinds of idola and "their belongings; all of which must be renounced and adjured "with a constant and solemn determination, and the intellect "entirely freed and purged from them; so that the approach to "the Kingdom of man, which is founded on the sciences, may be "like that of the Kingdom of Heaven, *into which none may enter* "*save in the character of a little child.*"[1]

Such earnestness of heart and consecration of intellect find expression in glowing eloquence, not spasmodic, but sustained and free. "*Eloquentia simulari non potest.*" Bacon had opportunities in many respects unique of leaving a splendid philosophical style in English literature. There can be but one beginning of anything; and Bacon was the pioneer of the new movement in science and philosophy. He was the herald of the new era and his mind and character were of the type to give it an imposing heralding. There is a great flourish of trumpets and extravagant display worthy the advent of the new age. Harvey hit off Bacon's characteristic manner when he said " he writes science like a Lord "Chancellor." It was this grasp and manner that made Bacon's exposition literature, while Harvey's *De Motu Sanguinis*, although it sets forth an infinitely better example of the new method than any Bacon gives, is merely of historical interest and that chiefly for the physiologist. Our author's mode of work is admirably indicated when he writes, " For were it not better for a man in a fair room to set up "one great light, or branching candlestick of lights, than to go about "with a small watch candle into every corner?"[2] His power was in the interpretation of the new spirit and the formulation of the new method in broad philosophical language, sweeping, eloquent, and impressive, such as that of the opening aphorism of the *Novum Organum*:—" Man, the servant and interpreter of nature, performs " and understands so much as he has collected concerning the order of

---

[1] *Novum Organum*, Book I., Aphorism lxviii.
[2] *Advancement*, Bk. I. (Works ed. by Ellis and Spedding), Vol. III., p. 286.

"nature by observation and reason : nor do his powers or his know-
"ledge extend further." It was far easier for Bacon to make a place,
and a glorious one, in literature with such a task than for his successors
to excel as writers, hampered as they were by the detailed and
laborious work of analysis and criticism. Locke could not have
filled Bacon's place, nor could the latter have achieved the former's
results in patient, lowly investigation. It was for Bacon to be
imaginative, majestic, and eloquent in a degree that has not been
possible for any philosopher or scientist since his day. His style is
therefore an isolated one. The typical English thinker has been of
the analytical, sceptical disposition. Bacon's mind was not of the
dissecting type; it could grasp wholes, vast wholes in one rapid comprehensive sweep. He gives us the results of the working of his own
genius; he rarely sets down logical, laborious processes with any
success. He is dictatorial, lordly, and oracular in his utterances.
He never argues; if he gives a reason it is in the form of a simile or
analogy.

The last general feature we shall notice in our author's style is the
division and arrangement he gives to his subjects. These, being loose
and unsystematic, are, on the whole, very unsatisfactory. His manner
of division is often too much governed by his artistic faculty, and his
arrangement and treatment are curious and arbitrary. This is perhaps
the greatest flaw in Bacon's writings, and is the feature in which
modern philosophical prose is so vastly superior to the early styles.
Quaintness of system is a feature of all Bacon's work. He was not
pre-eminently a close, logical reasoner, or an exact formulator. But
his mind was ever active, and he had remarkable powers of organization
and elaboration. Hence he must systematise whether he had satisfactory materials or not. Indeed, his schemes and plans went far in
advance of his materials, and were consequently very unreliable, and
are of little use to modern thought. Bacon's inventive genius and
power of constructive elaboration led him into great works that
produced very few results. The whole plan of the *Instauratio Magna* is
characterised rather by imposing conception than by feasibility. The
Advancement is, as regards arrangement, loose and ill-balanced, and its
treatment diffuse. Its beauty is of the rambling and profuse rather
than of the orderly and symmetrical type. In the *Novum Organum*
the division of the subject is largely mechanical, as with the form of
aphorism it was bound to be. It is a massive structure built of

curiously-figured blocks, but without any architectural subordination of parts to the whole.

One very marked feature of Bacon's style is the way in which a topic is started and skilfully broken up into divisions in the short space of a compact sentence. True, the division of a subject thus intuitively and rapidly arrived at has a greater artistic than logical worth; true, the division is generally arbitrary, but the artifice adds greatly to the order and clearness of the discourse. Almost all Bacon's arrangement and distribution of a subject is brought about with great artistic effect by the precision of a single word or a series of antithetical clauses. An illustration of the artistic method of arrangement will convey our meaning better than any description. In the *Advancement* order is got into a subject in the following ingenious and artistic manner :—

"There be therefore chiefly three vanities in studies, whereby "learning hath been traduced. For those things we do esteem "vain, which are either false or frivolous, those which either have "no truth or no use: and those persons we esteem vain, which "are either credulous or curious; and curiosity is either in "matter, or words: so that in reason as well as in experience, "there fall out to be these three distempers (as I may term them) "of learning; the first, fantastical learning; the second, con- "tentious learning; and the last, delicate learning; vain imagina- "tions, vain altercations, and vain affections; and with the last "I will begin."[1]

"This knowledge [*i.e.*, civil] hath three parts, according to "the three summary actions of society; which are Conversation, "Negotiation, and Government. For man seeketh in society "comfort, use, and protection: and they be three wisdoms of "divers natures, which do often sever; wisdom of the behaviour, "wisdom of business, and wisdom of state."[2]

Bacon touches nothing without dividing it up in this deft, quaint but artistic fashion.

(II.) Bacon's prose is figurative as no other English philosopher's has been. Perhaps the only philosopher with whom he may be compared in his constant use of figures, analogies, and illustrations is Plato. The latter was an artist, and his imagination and eloquence often ran away with his philosophy. Bacon also was a literary artist,

---

[1] *Advancement*, Bk. i. (Works), Vol. III., p. 282.
[2] *Ibid.*, Bk. ii. (Works), Vol. III., p. 445.

"For to say that a blind custom of obedience should be a surer obligation than duty taught and understood, it is to affirm that a blind man may tread surer by a guide than a seeing man can by a light."[1]

"So it is in contemplation; if a man will begin with certainties, he shall end in doubts; but if he will be content to begin with doubts, he shall end in certainties."[2]

"Nevertheless I shall yield, that he that cannot contract the sight of his mind as well as disperse and dilate it, wanteth a great faculty."[3]

The above are taken from the *Advancement*. All the Aphorisms of the First Book of the *Novum Organum* are more or less of this nature.

The second form of sentence is the one by which Bacon acquires greatest dignity and power of eloquence. It is of the elaborated and balanced form, making use of antitheses. The period is launched, and carried forward by a series of co-ordinate phrases or clauses, of close correspondence in form and sound, until we come to a clause which, both by form and thought, marks the middle or fulcrum of the sentence; then we proceed with a balancing series of opposing co-ordinate phrases, and the whole sentence is finished off with a pompous turn. The following, which is one of Bacon's finest and richest passages, is an instance of this most careful and dignified composition :—

"But the greatest error of all the rest is the mistaking or misplacing of the last or furthest end of knowledge. For men have entered into a desire of learning and knowledge, sometimes upon a natural curiosity and inquisitive appetite; sometimes to entertain their minds with variety and delight; sometimes for ornament and reputation; and sometimes to enable them to victory of wit and contradiction; and most times for lucre and profession; and seldom sincerely to give a true account of their gift of reason, to the benefit and use of men: as if there were sought in knowledge a couch, whereupon to rest a searching and restless spirit; or a terrace, for a wandering and variable mind to walk up and down with a fair prospect; or a tower of state,

---

[1] *Advancement*, Bk. i. (Works), Vol. III., p. 273.
[2] *Ibid.*, Bk. ii., p. 293.
[3] *Ibid.*, Bk. ii., p. 279.

"for a proud mind to raise itself upon ; or a fort or commanding ground, for strife and contention ; or a shop, for profit or sale ; and not a rich storehouse, for the glory of the Creator, and the relief of man's estate." [1]

The following are also good instances of Bacon's periodic style. They contain some of his most important philosophical statements:—

"But the conduct of mankind has hitherto been such, that it is no wonder nature has not opened herself to them. For the information of the senses is treacherous and deceitful; observation careless, irregular, and accidental ; tradition idle, rumorous, and vain; practice narrow and servile; experience blind, stupid, vague and broken ; and natural history extremely light and empty: wretched materials for the understanding to fashion into philosophy and the sciences!" [2]

"But the most difficult part of our task consists in the form of induction, and the judgment to be made by it; for that form of the logicians which proceeds by simple enumeration, is a childish thing, concludes unsafely, lies open to contradictory instances, and regards only common matters; yet determines nothing: whilst the sciences require such a form of induction, as can separate, adjust, and verify experience, and come to a necessary determination by proper exclusions and rejections." [3]

"The human intellect is not of the character of a dry light, but receives a tincture from the will and affections, which generates 'sciences after its own will'; for man more readily believes what he wishes to be true. And so it rejects difficult things, from impatience of enquiry:—sober things, because they narrow hope;—the deeper things of nature, from superstition;—the light of experience, from arrogance and disdain, lest the mind should seem to be occupied with worthless and changing matters;—paradoxes, from a fear of the opinion of the vulgar:—in short, the affections enter and corrupt the intellect in innumerable ways, and these sometimes imperceptible." [4]

"Those however who aspire not to guess and divine, but to discover and know; who propose not to divise mimic and

---

[1] *Advancement*, Bk. i. (Works), Vol. III., p. 294.
[2] *Distributio Operis*.
[3] *Ibid.*
[4] *Novum Organum*, Bk. i., Aph. xlix.

"fabulous worlds of their own, but to examine and dissect the nature of this real world itself; must go to facts themselves for everything."[1]

Perhaps no English writer, except Shakespeare, has had such sustained popularity and wide-spread influence as Bacon. His optimism, and the eloquence to which it gave rise, have proved an ever fresh source of inspiration for mankind. Whatever we may think of certain of his actions, there is no breath of insincerity or meanness throughout his pages. The dignity of his spirit has revealed itself through his speech, and has influenced all who have listened to his words. He has roused by majestic eloquence, he has impressed by incisiveness of utterance, he has moved by simple earnestness of tone. No man has ever had more unhesitating confidence in his own message, more robust hope for the future of knowledge and of mankind, or more irresistible enthusiasm for the cause of science; and certainly no man has written in a manner more calculated to elevate or to inspire than the great seer who adopted as his prophecy, "*Multi pertransibunt et augebitur scientia.*"

---

[1] *Distributio Operis* (Works), Vol. IV., p. 28.

II.

Thomas Hobbes.

THOMAS HOBBES is an isolated figure alike in English philosophy and in English literature. He holds a unique position in both. No man ever thought like Hobbes, and certainly no English prose possesses in an equal degree those qualities for which his writings are remarkable. The effects of temperament on philosophy and on style are clearly traceable in the case of Hobbes. The positive traits of his character are the index to the peculiarity of his thought; the limitations of his personality correspond to and cause the marked defects of his intellectual scheme of things: philosophy and disposition are the key to his style. Given his sentiments, his literary medium, though so remarkable, is naturalness itself; the character of his thought being what it was, his style ought to be just what we find it.

The name "Hobbist" carries with it, perhaps, as much ill odour as any that a philosopher has given to a body of tenets or to a school of thought. To most Englishmen of the seventeenth century "Hobbist" was as significant as "Epicurean." Nor is it easy to rescue the true personality of Hobbes from the clouds of political and theological prejudice in which the times enveloped him. But we cannot bring ourselves to think that his personality was at all an attractive or a lovable one. Those who valued him did so because of the robust strength and originality of his thought, his keen wit, and his intense utterance. His opinions were very decided and distinctive; his views such as to shock conventional minds; and his asseverations forceful even to violence. His friend Aubrey has a very significant remark about him. Referring to his life after the Restoration, he says, " The " witts at Court were wont to bayte him. But he feared none of them, " and would make his part good. The king would call him *the beare* : " ' Here comes the beare to be bayted' ! "

In disposition, as well as in general tone of speculation, Hobbes reminds us greatly of Bentham. The qualities of his character, with one exception, are all on the side of strength and ruggedness. This one exception was a constitutional timorousness that rendered him little more than a coward in the face of physical danger and social unrest. Such a failing is the more remarkable when we remember the daring and the uncompromising nature of his thought. He was intellectually fearless, fond of paradox, and severely logical. His thought was massive, his intellect was vigorous, and his ideas and principles were grasped in the vice-like clutches of his strenuous mind. Devoid of sentiment and of imagination, he was utterly unsympathetic towards, and unresponsive to the more tender, as also to the more noble aspects of human life. He was unemotional, with the exception that he was at times irate. Harsh and unexpansive, self-assertive and dictatorial, haughty and contradictious, he might well be considered by many repulsive and perverse. Certainly there is nothing gracious or idealistic about the man. He was self-centred, and was never free from the prudential dictates of a calculating and a quiet-loving mind, rendered nervous by natural timidity. The cold, unsympathetic, unimpulsive cast of his disposition is indicated by the fact that when England was given up to parties and to strife he was neither a thorough-going Royalist nor a Revolutionist, neither a Puritan nor an Anglican. He quoted scripture, yet in such a way that men said he was an irreverent rationalist. He protested his religious faith, yet he was put down as an atheist. Unlike so many others, he was not carried away by the current of events, and was, by his dispassionate view of the situation, saved from becoming an ephemeral politician or an enthusiastic patriot. While other men, his friends, staked their life on their opinions, he retired abroad to cultivate the philosophic calm, and treated the questions of the day, not as questions of a day, but in so comprehensive a manner, and with such a rational setting and logical coherence, that his works remain a lasting monument of English speculative literature.

Hobbes's philosophy is a reflection of his own character in all its strength, ruggedness, and rigid limitations. The centre of his interest in these tumultuous times was the study of human nature, for knowledge of human nature alone could give the solution to the political and religious difficulties of the country. But it was unfortunate for his philosophical analysis of human nature that he was himself such a one-sided specimen of humanity. There is much truth in Clarendon's remark: "Mr. Hobbes having taken upon himself to imitate God, and "created Man after his own likeness, given him all the passions and "affections which he finds in himself, and no other, he prescribes him "the judge of all things and words, according to the definitions he sets "down, with the Authority of a Creator."

The man who, with such decided opinions on social and political problems, amidst such stirring and exciting times as the Civil Wars, could retire to France and frame a cool, self-consistent, thoroughly grounded philosophy, comprehensive in grasp and of universal scope, must needs have been endowed with a peculiarly philosophical temperament. The result is a magnificent sweep of survey, and a logical continuity and completeness of system manifested in his works at a time when these qualities were least to be expected; a speculative grasp to which we have no parallel in English systems until the "Synthetic Philosophy" of Herbert Spencer.

No doubt Hobbes's speculations were very profoundly affected by the momentous affairs that were being transacted in the English nation. But the marvel is that we can read the philosophical portions of his writings with so little consciousness of what was going on around him. How intense and eloquent, even fierce, Milton becomes amidst the same scenes! Men were fighting for their dearest liberties; religious feeling was stirred to its very depths. Almost all the literary productions of such periods bear ineradicable marks of special and accidental circumstances. In Hobbes, though the problems of the times gave a cue to his theories, there is remarkably little trace of local and temporal colouring. It needs strong grasp of comprehensive principles and able mastery in systematic construction, to realize, as Hobbes did, that it is impossible to get a thoroughgoing, well-grounded conception of society—the great Leviathan—and an insight into the conditions of its welfare, without an intimate knowledge of its "matter" and "artificer," "both which is man," and an analysis of his powers, physical, mental, and moral. But the study of man as part of the physical world presupposes an adequate physical science. Hence Hobbes developed a mechanical atomism. Beyond this again we must have a "first philosophy" comprehending mathematics. And since no science can be formulated, no investigations carried on, without certain presuppositions and fundamental principles, he begins with logic and a formulation of method. Here we have unusual breadth of view and unity of system. The methods of explanation are few and simple, the thought is coherent and harmonious, and the theory is well compacted. As a mere attempt at exhaustive and comprehensive system, Hobbes's work is masterly.

Although considerable disorganization resulted in the order in which our author's books appeared, owing to the pressure of contemporary events calling for his political opinions first; and although there is some complication arising from the fact that certain works were written originally in English and duplicates afterwards made in Latin, while others were written in Latin and translations made in English, yet if we bear in mind the general plan of his system it is easy to find our whereabouts in these voluminous productions. The logical scheme of his construction is, first, De Corpore; second, De Homine; third, De Cive. These three divisions give the titles to the three Latin works which contain the formal exposition of his doctrines. He had planned out on these lines his far-reaching philosophy before he began to write his particular works. Moreover, although the interest of political events in England led to the publication of what was really the last complement of his theories, the work on Government, *De Cive*, first, yet he had already not only planned and elaborated the foundations on which this top stone rested, but actually written in English that part of his theory which dealt with human nature and social life. For in 1640 there was privately circulated a manuscript copy (in two parts) of what was afterwards published as the English works, *Human Nature* and *De Corpore Politico*. The *De Cive* published as a Latin work in 1642 corresponds to *De Corpore Politico*. The first and second parts of the formal Latin exposition appeared as *De Corpore* in 1655 and *De Homine* in 1658. This last, however, was a mere formal completion of his promised system, and is of little value as compared with the English work *Human Nature*. The *Human Nature* and *De Corpore Politico*, which had formed the little treatise of 1640, were published in 1650. They formed two parts of Hobbes's so-called English "tripos." The third part of this "tripos" is *Of Liberty and Necessity*, a theological discussion of freewill. But by far the most popular and most influential of Hobbes's writings is the *Leviathan*, an English work published in 1651. It was a direct appeal to the English nation, and contains most of his important theories. Even if our object were an investigation of Hobbes's distinctive doctrines, we might almost restrict ourselves to the *Human Nature*, the *De Corpore Politico*, and the *Leviathan*. The *De Corpore* cannot be regarded as English literature. It was written in Latin, and its interest is rather for natural than for mental or social philosophy. The chapters on Logic, on Method, and on Sensation, however, are important as shewing how the author passes, by his mechanical atomism, without a break, from the material to the mental world.

The three English works, *Human Nature*, *De Corpore Politico*, and *Leviathan*, are written in Hobbes's characteristic style. As regards the *Leviathan*, the strictly philosophical matter is contained in the first two parts, the last two being political and theological. The author's aim in writing it was to give a succinct and effective account of his views on the organization and government of Church and State, prefaced by such a groundwork as was necessary to give these views a scientific and philosophical support. It is this groundwork that contains Hobbes's philosophy. The *Human Nature* and *De Corpore Politico* are a little freer in the exposition of some points than the *Leviathan*. The sentences are slightly longer, and the language not quite so severe. But there is very little variation in our author's prose, and its remarkable uniformity makes it possible to appreciate the features of his style from an examination of any page chosen at random.

Hobbes developed his system chiefly under the stimulating influence of Continental thought. The encouragement and patronage given to him by the physical investigators and scholars of Paris enabled him to see that his doctrines were of interest to the scientific world. He had spent many years of study in the acquisition of a Latin style, and he had aided Bacon himself in the expression of his thoughts in that language. It thus appeared natural to him that the formal exposition of his doctrines should be in Latin. But it was an age of polemics, and Hobbes had very definite and valuable views with which he desired to influence the government and religion of England. It was this that drew him from the more exclusive and select audience of the learned into English literature, that he might appeal to the English nation. Hobbes, indeed, had much more faith in his native tongue as a repository for permanent thought than Bacon. And this was very natural, when we consider how much more reliable and how much less quaint English becomes in the prose of Hobbes than in that of any of his predecessors.

Hobbes's prose style is one of the most striking and effective to be found in the language. Perhaps no philosopher has propounded his views in so clear and forceful a manner. The energy, precision, and lucidity of the medium proceed from great force of personal character and very distinctive doctrines. The feeling we experience in reading Hobbes is like that of plunging into cold, clear, limpid water on a summer day. It is bracing and invigorating, and we are at once active and alert. Certainly the temperature is low, and inclined to be chill; but that only increases the vigour. The prose is remarkably uniform, and we have none of the intricate tangles of clauses, parentheses, and involved subordinate sentences, which so greatly mar Elizabethan writings. The sentences are direct, perspicuous, and well constructed. The diction is luminous, the phrases happy and well rounded, the sentences terse. Hobbes never beats the air; his clauses and sentences fall like hammer-strokes; each has a purpose and each fulfils it. The following passages will enable us to realize these properties of our author's prose better than any description:

"Whatsoever therefore is consequent to a time of war, when "every man is enemy to every man, the same is consequent to "the time wherein men live without other security than what "their own strength and their own invention shall furnish them "withal. In such condition there is no place for industry, because "the fruit thereof is uncertain, and consequently no culture of the "earth; no navigation, nor use of the commodities that may be "imported by sea; no commodious building; no instruments of "moving and removing such things as require much force; no "knowledge of the face of the earth; no account of time; no "arts; no letters; no society; and, which is worst of all, continual fear and danger of violent death; and the life of man "solitary, poor, nasty, brutish, and short."[1]

"The 'value,' or 'worth' of a man, is as of all other things, "his price; that is to say, so much as would be given for the use "of his power: and therefore is not absolute; but a thing "dependent on the need and judgment of another. An able "conductor of soldiers is of great price in time of war present, or "imminent; but in peace not so. A learned and uncorrupt judge, "is much worth in time of peace; but not so much in war. And "as in other things, so in men, not the seller, but the buyer

---

[1] *Leviathan*, Pt. i., Ch. xiii. (Molesworth's Ed.), p. 113.

"determines the price. For let a man, as most men do, rate themselves at the highest value they can; yet their true value is no more than it is esteemed by others."[1]

We have noticed that Hobbes's writings manifest great constructive power and a comprehensiveness of mind that is unsurpassed. His, however, was not a breadth of view that demanded, or gave scope for, eloquence as did Bacon's, whose horizon was glorious chiefly because it was a distant one. It was no longer possible for thinkers to spend time upon the threshold of knowledge and enlarge upon the potentialities of science. Hobbes had an intensely concrete and practical mind, and was sure to betake himself to a specific, matter-of-fact style. His subject might be abstract, but he always had something very particular and practical to say about it. His success is usually just at the point where Bacon failed, namely, the application of broad principles and general methods to important details. Hence his style is direct, precise, and plain, and is devoid of that pompous grandeur and glowing eloquence in which Bacon revelled. It is in the tangible and the concrete, rather than in the vague and the visionary, that Hobbes finds subjects most adapted to his genius and his style. Bacon throws around his subjects a halo of glory and romance: Hobbes presents his object in all its angularity and literalness. But in swift, striking analysis, in orderly, compressed, effective exposition, and in the forceful driving home of practical conclusions, Hobbes excels. While Bacon is surveying a new territory and expatiating upon the grandeur of the scene, Hobbes has sunk his shaft and got his ore.

A great deal of the energy and force of our author's style is due to his pugnacity. He does not assume the attitude of conciliation or compromise. He ever shows a warlike front; and anything that can be gained by audacity is his. He rarely, in his writings, relies on our sympathy; he never courts it. His attitude is either offensive or defensive; he never studies persuasion. He adopts the harsh, unconciliating manner calculated first to arouse, then to overcome opposition. Nor is the exposition less dogmatic than pugnacious. He is fond of decisive utterance, sweeping statement, and iron-wrought definition. He never suggests, never implies, never even discusses; there is hardly a sustained, all-round argument in the whole of his writings. Every subject is treated in the same dictatorial, legislative,

---

[1] *Leviathan*, Pt. i., Ch. x. (Molesworth's Ed.), p. 76.

cut-and-dried way. The result is a precision, a deliberateness, and a strength that are unsurpassed in the English language.

The luminousness and plausibility of our author's style are due largely to his extreme nominalist position. Human knowledge is, for Hobbes, contained in the import of words. Define clearly what you mean by common words, and the end of philosophy is accomplished. That human thought has to penetrate below the surface of language, and to spend its best energies in laying bare what common speech has concealed; and that the results of our thought are often very difficult to express in common words; these are things that Hobbes never dreamed of. Instead of subtle metaphysical and psychological analyses, we have the rough and ready way of nominalism, with its crude distinctions. Instead of freeing thought from the conventionalities and perversities of common speech, and leaving definitions as the final product of speculation, Hobbes tries to build up a philosophy out of arbitrary definitions of every-day terms. This forms a very ready means of obtaining an easily intelligible and plausible style, and obviates the necessity of severe analysis. But it leaves the prose devoid of suppleness and flexibility. Many sections are little more than dictionaries of a particular class of common words; the peculiarity being, that these are chosen so as to hang together by a common tie, and defined on a principle that makes them appear to fall into a most natural system. The following quotations will illustrate this coherent, luminous style of descriptive definition. They are from the tenth chapter, Part i., of *Leviathan*, which is composed of a series of definitions on the notions "power," "worth," "dignity," and "honour."

"To pray to another, for aid of any kind, is 'to honour'; because
"a sign we have an opinion he has power to help; and the more
"difficult the aid is, the more is the honour.

"To obey, is to honour, because no man obeys them whom they
"think have no power to help, or hurt them. And consequently
"to disobey, is to 'dishonour.'

"To give great gifts to a man, is to honour him; because it is
"buying of protection, and acknowledging of power. To give little
"gifts, is to dishonour; because it is but alms, and signifies an
"opinion of the need of small helps.

"To be sedulous in promoting another's good, also to flatter,
"is to honour; as a sign we seek his protection or aid. To
"neglect, is to dishonour.

"To give way or place to another, in any commodity, is to
"honour; being a confession of greater power. To arrogate, is to
"dishonour.

"To shew any sign of love, or fear of another, is to honour; for
"both to love, and to fear, is to value. To contemn, or less to
"love or fear than he expects, is to dishonour; for it is under-
"valueing.

"To praise, magnify, or call happy, is to honour; because
"nothing but goodness, power, and felicity is valued. To revile,
"mock, or pity, is to dishonour."[1]

Many of the admirable qualities of our author's style—energy, emphasis, and clinching terseness—are due to the narrowness of the track along which his thought travels. His pointed prose pierces its way like a plough. Concentration of thought leads to intensity and compression of utterance; exaggeration of conception invariably adds force to style; while one-sided aspects are invariably clearer and better defined than complex situations. It is comparatively easy to give vivid exposition to partial thought. Hobbes's view is only of one side in everything, and it is ever the same side. Hence the consistency and plausibility of his writing, even when he is making most outrageous statements. It is often his calm audacity in exaggeration that wins him success. His statement is so penetrating, so bold, so unfaltering, that there is not the slightest hint of a suspicion that things can be, or can be expressed otherwise. Simplicity of enunciation is with Hobbes frequently the result of artificial simplicity of conception. Hobbes does not attempt to explain reality in all its elaborate intricacies. He makes an abstract case by suppressing all complicating elements, perplexing details, and modifying factors. Weigh, balance, argue, Hobbes never does. Throughout the entire extent of his works there is little amplification, little thorough, all-round handling. Hence the more we know of him the more dogmatic he appears, and the more we see wherein the fascination of his style lies, the less plausible does his case become. It is the strength and clearness of his prose that makes his doctrines not only tolerable but apparently feasible. Every position is won by the force of an individual sentence, and that force is so great that unless we are aroused we do not feel inclined to contest it. Hence the danger of such a style as Hobbes's. It is not a vague misty effusion, which, producing no conviction, we

---

[1] *Leviathan*, Pt. i., Ch. x. (Molesworth's Ed.), pp. 76, 7.

allow to dissipate: it is so penetrating, its movement so quick and sure, and its action so effective, that we are either overborne or need to brace ourselves against the shock. It is a prose that cannot be ignored. Hobbes does not compose for cumulative effect, he never piles on words, phrases, or sentences: he never uses two words where one will do, and he is extremely economical in the use of his adjectives. Says Hallam, " His language is so lucid and concise that it would be " almost as improper to put an algebraical process in different terms as " some of his metaphysical paragraphs." He has a truly wonderful power of setting an aspect of truth in a striking light, sharply defined, exaggerated, unnaturally simple, bare and unadorned. His expressions are striking, his phrases well knit, and his sentences naturally form themselves into ringing maxims and epigrammatic utterances.

" The felicity of this life consisteth not in the repose of a mind " satisfied." [1]

" For benefits oblige, and obligation is thraldom; and unre-" quitable obligation perpetual thraldom; which is to one's equals " hateful." [2]

" The sum of virtue is to be sociable with them that will be " sociable, and formidable to them that will not." [3]

" Experience concludeth nothing universally." [4]

" To honour those another honours, is to honour him." [5]

But in spite of all Hobbes's precision and apparent exactness, his prose suffers much from a lack of exact technical terms to serve as moorings for his speculations. It was quite in harmony with his general philosophical position for him to reject utterly the technical language of the schools, and adopt concrete every-day words wherewith to express his doctrines. One unfortunate result of the absence of a technical and exact nomenclature is a very perplexing indecision when he is on the borderland between the physical and the mental; and though Hobbes almost invariably chooses a materialistic interpretation, yet there is often a regrettable lack of explicitness on the subject resulting from a want of philosophical terms. If thought is too refined and abstract for ordinary language we begin to be absurd, according to

---

[1] *Leviathan*, Pt. i., Ch. xi. (Molesworth's Ed.), p. 85.
[2] *Ibid.*, p. 87.
[3] *De Corpore Politico*, Ch. iv., Sec. 15.
[4] *Human Nature*, Ch. iv., Sec. 16.
[5] *Leviathan*, Pt. i., Ch. x. (Molesworth's Ed.), p. 78.

Hobbes. He therefore rejects the terminology of the Schoolmen, and tries to convey his doctrines in common speech. As a result he often has to take refuge in vague, fantastic modes of expression, and there is at times much obscurity and indefiniteness due to the lack of a fixed, technical vocabulary wherewith to replace the dog-Latin of Scholasticism.

The following are some of the rather extravagant words made to do service for "sensation"—"phantom," "appearance," "apparition," "image." Again the rest of knowledge, which is not sensation, is called indiscriminately "images," "fancies," "representations," "phantasy," "ideas." Sentences like the following can hardly be termed precise. "The imagery and representation of the qualities of the thing without, "is that we call our conception, imagination, ideas, notice or know- "ledge of them."

Another example of looseness where there is need of an exact nomenclature is seen in his use of the word "fancy," which in Hobbes's prose is often raised to the rank of a technical term— ". . . the sight, the colour, the idea of it in the fancy." (Here "fancy" equals sensation or imagination) : " . . . by which is "meant . . . a good fancy." (Here "fancy" is synonymous with "wit"): " . . . judgment does all, except sometimes the under- "standing have need to be opened by some apt similitude : and then "there is so much use of fancy." (Here "fancy" refers to the power of using analogy or simile.)

Hobbes's manner of exposition is such, that the attainable degree of refinement and subtlety of thought is limited by the comparative rigidity of his medium. Further, anything but crude analysis was impossible until a finer technical instrument had been fashioned. The language of unsophisticated thought was gradually found powerless to grip the subtle and elusive questions of psychology and metaphysics. And just as the development of Logic as a Science by Aristotle, necessitated the invention of a logical technique, so the growth of psychological analysis has necessitated the formation of a more discriminating nomenclature for mental facts. We shall find that in Locke and in Hume, English prose gained much in suppleness and flexibility, but little in technical exactness. It is to the influence of German writers that we owe the superior capacity of the present-day English for philosophical expression.

There is one very important feature of Hobbes's style, which has been dwelt upon by Hallam, namely its uniformity. "Hobbes," says this authority, "is perhaps the first of whom we can strictly say that "he is a good English writer, for the excellent passages of Hooper, "Sidney, Raleigh, Bacon, Taylor, Chillingworth, and others of the "Elizabethan or the first Stuart period are not sufficient to establish "their claim, a good writer being one whose composition is nearly "uniform, and who never sinks to such inferiority as we must confess "in most of these." That Hobbes's prose is exceptionally regular is manifest; whether it is not too uniform for a perfect prose style is less easily settled. The originality and force of his language, together with the striking novelty of his thoughts, do much to keep us interested and on the alert; but as far as the style is concerned there is little variety, and the regularity amounts almost to monotony. If Hobbes surpasses Bacon in the mean level of excellence of composition, as he no doubt does, yet Bacon far outstrips him in the artistic variety of his sentences. Hobbes never rises to the pitch of a periodic style, and is thus denied all the higher reaches of prose. He possesses no feeling strong enough to force him out of his usual even pace. This may be admirable for *his* philosophy, but it places very serious limitations to the possibilities of prose. We must not hesitate, however, to pay him the honour due to the great forerunner, in point of regularity and reliability, of the classic prose of later times. He has written a philosophical prose that reads more like modern writing than any other of this period. But Hobbes could attain to nothing of the polish and artistic manipulation of Berkeley. The excellences of his style are not sufficiently varied; strength and force prevail to such an extent as to leave no place for finer, subtler, and nobler qualities. It would have been a great gain not only to his style, but indirectly to his philosophy, if Hobbes had at times broken away from the regular pattern of his ordinary prose. All topics cannot be dealt with in a cast-iron, dogmatic, forceful fashion; and there is much in speculative thought and in human nature that demands refined and artistic treatment, much that may call for eloquence and lofty periods.

Cognate with this lack of range and want of elevation is the utter absence of the imaginative element. Hobbes's constructive power, within the sphere of thought his mind can compass, is very great indeed. But his genius is for the concrete, the tangible, the practical, the materialistic. He has no metaphysical imagination; hence his philosophy is confined to the common-sense view of mundane affairs.

He finds an ultimate solution in mechanical atomism. Here there is no demand and no scope for imagination or fertile fancy. The highest attainment in this direction is ingenuity in the construction of theories and of working hypotheses. Such opinions and such gifts of mind have very decided effects on style. While Bacon's imagination was ever shewing itself, even in his driest mood, in the most picturesque analogies, luxuriant figures, and charming fancies, Hobbes regards the appearance in philosophy of a figure or any colouring of feeling or imagination as an impertinence. If he ever does slip into figurative speech, there is such a sober, quakerish air that we feel impressed that it is not to be taken as ornament, but as an aid to the understanding. The illustrations and analogies he allows himself are singularly happy and ingenious. They are always apt, stick close to the sense, and assist rather than divert the mind. We will give some instances of his illustrative power :—

"For thoughts are to the desires, as scouts and spies, to range "abroad and find the way to things desired." [1]

"As standing water put into motion by the stroke of a stone, "or blast of wind, doth not presently give over moving as soon as "the wind ceaseth, or the stone settleth, so neither doth the "effect cease which the object hath wrought upon the brain, so "soon as by the turning aside of the organs the object ceaseth to "work ; that is to say, though the sense be past, the image or "conception remaineth." [2]

"Such are commonly the thoughts of men, that are not only "without company, but also without care of anything; though "even then their thoughts are as busy as at other times, but "without harmony ; as the sound which a lute out of tune would "yield to any man ; or in tune, to one that could not play. And "yet in this wild ranging of the mind, a man may oft-times per-"ceive the way of it, and the dependence of one thought upon "another. For in a discourse of our present civil war, what could "be more impertinent than to ask, as one did, what was the value "of a Roman penny ? Yet the coherence to me was manifest "enough. For the thought of the war introduced the thought of "the delivering up of the king to his enemies ; the thought of "that brought in the thought of the delivering up of Christ ; and

---

[1] *Leviathan*, Pt. i., Ch. viii. (Molesworth's Ed.), p. 61.
[2] *Human Nature*, Ch. iii., p. 9 (Molesworth's Ed.).

"that again the thought of the thirty pence, which was the price of that treason; and thence easily followed that malicious question; and all this in a moment of time, for thought is quick."[1]

The following shews Hobbes at his best in the use of figure and contains a rare gem :—

"Nature itself cannot err; and as men abound in copiousness of language, so they become more wise, or more mad than ordinary. Nor is it possible without letters to become either excellently wise, or, unless his memory be hurt by disease or ill constitution of organs, excellently foolish. For words are wise men's counters, they do but reckon by them: but they are the money of fools, that value them by the authority of an Aristotle, a Cicero, or a Thomas, or any other doctor whatsoever, if but a man."[2]

We find no pleasant wit sparkling in Hobbes's pages, though there is at times an undercurrent of sarcasm beneath his serious sentiments. The following is typical :—

"A democracy, in effect, is no more than an aristocracy of orators, interrupted sometimes with the temporary monarchy of one orator."[3]

Hobbes was a most careful composer, and never allows anything slovenly to pass his pen. He attained to a clear-cut precision and lucidity of style that we can never too much admire. But there was that in the man himself and in his peculiar doctrines which excluded from his writing one half of the qualities which it is possible for prose to possess. There is a harshness and ruggedness that defies the approach of beauty; a force that spurns persuasion; an unyielding rigour that despises the smooth arts of eloquence. And can we wonder that Hobbes should be all unconscious of the finer, the nobler, and the more artistic resources of speech when it is a rank materialistic conception of the universe he has to expound, a mechanical atomism as the last word to offer; and as low an estimate of human nature to propound as ever philosopher has had the impudence to ask humanity to accept as an appreciation of itself? Just as certainly as doubt brings with it paralysis and pessimism spells despair, materialism acts as a clog and a low standard of human nature as a degradation and a blight to

---

[1] *Leviathan*, Pt. i., Ch. iii., p. 12 (Molesworth's Ed.).
[2] *Ibid.*, Pt. i., Ch. iv., p. 25 (Molesworth's Ed.).
[3] *De Corpore Politico*, Pt. ii., Ch. ii., Sec. 5.

literature. Here are some of the chief items of Hobbes's account of the nature and constitution of man, of knowledge, and of society:—

"Sense, therefore, is some internal motion in the sentient." "Imagination is decaying sense." "Reasoning is reckoning" and of the nature of "adding and subtracting." "The *alternate succes-* "*sion of appetite and fear* . . . is that we call *deliberation.*" "In "deliberation, the last appetite, as also the last fear, is called *will.*" "The wills of most men are governed only by fear." "Such a liberty "as is free from necessity, is not to be found in the will either of men "or beasts." "Every man doth in all his voluntary actions intend "some good unto himself." "No man giveth, but with intention of "good to himself." "The desire of injuring is innate in all. Man is "to man a wolf." "Seeing then to the offensiveness of every man's "nature one to another, there is added a right of every man to every- "thing . . . the estate of men in this natural liberty, is the estate "of war." "The natural state of man is non-moral, unregulated: "moral rules are means to the end of peace, which is a means to the "end of self-preservation."

Can any man be an inspiring advocate who intends to teach such beliefs? It was only a Hobbes who could conceive them and adhere to them. In no one else's hands could they have been made to appear anything but hateful.

Idealism may not be true, but if Hobbism be a realistic and satisfactory account of the nature and capacity of man as he is or ever has been, then human nature is no theme for literature. M. Taine says of Hobbes, "He wiped out from the heart all noble and refined "sentiments"; "he cuts as with a surgeon's knife at the heart of the "most living creeds." And along with such clearance of all noble and refined sentiment goes all hope of noble and refined language. He puts an ignoble, mechanical interpretation on everything of which he desires an explanation, and invariably chooses the most frigid and passionless language in which to express it. Wherever there might be room for poetry, sentiment, or elevated feeling in the interpretation of nature or man, knowledge or morals, there is an exhibition of the wires and mechanism of a most unlovely working model. The richer and more mellow qualities of literary style are not called for in expounding a philosophy of levers, and pulleys, and wooden theories, and artificial definitions. Hobbes represents reality not in its natural delicate shades, but in pigments crude and glaring. We find no twilight effects in his scenes. Every object must submit to the scorching blaze of noonday. There is no attempt to drape the baldness and angularity of his extremely logical and formal conceptions. There is no charm of art, no allurements of imagination, no glow of eloquence, no sway of periods, no lofty heart-stirring appeal. The life and vigour so manifest do not produce profusion or richness. The style would spurn such prodigal waste. All is cold as ice, automatic as a machine. Hobbes's thought comes as if frozen into the very sentences that contain it.

III.

John Locke.

THE name of John Locke marks an era in more than one department of modern thought. His works on religious toleration, politics, education, and philosophy are landmarks in the several provinces to which they belong. The *Essay concerning Human Understanding*, as his great work is modestly entitled, is the book of books in our speculative literature. Its author was a typical Englishman, endowed richly with prudence and common sense, and manifesting an extreme dislike of paradoxes and a keen appetite for facts. As a thinker, he had a natural aversion to all theories of an imaginative and far-fetched character, a suspicion of vast, artificial systems, a hatred of all intellectual sham, and a scientific mind to the extent of preferring one fact to a whole world of theory. He was a passionless, reasonable, pious man whose infatuation for truth was matched by a sustained, practical zeal for liberty of thought and the progress of knowledge. It was truth, whatever that might prove to be, from the pursuit of which neither personal vanity nor the heat of argument ever diverted him. Though a thinker of great originality and power, he was wanting in constructive genius. He was no system-builder, and was apt to be satisfied with fragmentary truth. By an intellect solid rather than brilliant, cautious and practical rather than daring or visionary, he contributed much towards the elucidation of those problems to the solution of which he set himself. He was an unostentatious worker whose influence has been due entirely to genuine power of thought. Such a man could not be a metaphysician, but he excelled as an empirical psychologist. Voltaire, when giving his impressions of England, wrote:—" Such a Multitude of Reasoners " having written a Romance of the Soul, a Sage at last arose, who " gave, with an Air of the greatest Modesty, the History of it. Mr. " Locke has display'd the Human Soul, in the same manner as an " excellent Anatomist explains the Springs of the human Body."[1] Thus when Locke essays to examine human knowledge, it is not in

---

[1] *Voltaire's Letters concerning the English Nation* (English, 1733), Letter No. xiii.

order to erect a system, or to perform anything of a very brilliant or astounding character, but simply to find out the way where truth lies and to lay bare and exterminate some of the roots of prejudice and error.

Locke may be said to have begun the modern systematic study of the human mind and its contents. In such empirical investigation by introspection he excelled; and his research resulted in the most thorough and elaborate account of the human understanding that had as yet been given. Really to appreciate the literary style in which Locke carried out his work, we must consider it with constant reference to the peculiar character of his undertaking. It is, indeed, a significant fact that the man who holds a foremost place in the history of English philosophy, is usually assigned so unenviable a position in the history of our literature. And this is the more noteworthy when we consider that, excepting only Bunyan's *Pilgrim's Progress*, Locke's *Essay concerning Human Understanding* is the single great masterpiece of the last part of the Seventeenth Century; and that, as a speculative treatise, it has had a unique fortune in point of popularity and widespread, definite influence. The explanation usually given for such literary depreciation of Locke is, that the value of the *Essay* lies chiefly in the originality and worth of the thought, and that with this literature has no concern. But even if a clear line could be drawn between the manner and matter of an art, yet it would appear a bad principle of criticism to consider the mode of expression or the plan of construction of a piece of literature without any reference to the character of the thought. The form of the Epic, as contrasted with that of the Sonnet, is determined by the subject. Are we, then, to expect in philosophical prose those qualities which are suitable for the style of a light Essay or a Romance? But the average literary savant abominates the very name of philosophy, and has little interest in what appear to him its dry-as-dust discussions. In such cases there is scant justice done to those literary features most essential to the exposition of abstract and difficult thought. Speculative writings have seriously suffered by the unsympathetic handling of men whose one idea is artistic production. Locke's *Essay* has been no exception, though in many respects it least deserves it, for Locke did his utmost to make it palatable. But if the unwilling critic plods religiously through its pages, he probably takes his revenge by dubbing its style "dull," "monotonous," "humdrum," "bald," "inelegant," "crabbed," "bad." Such terms are considered quite adequate to characterise some of the world's greatest philosophical masterpieces by critics who do not shew the least appreciation of the requirements of a philosophical prose. But is it not folly to consign Aristotle, Kant, and Locke to literary perdition? A great teacher of philosophy may, and probably will, lack certain powers of execution most admired and affected by the *littérateur*, but there are others of which he must not be destitute, namely, those peculiarly demanded by the nature of his subject-matter. It might be admitted that, judged by the ideal of pure literature, the above epithets, as applied to Locke's style, are justifiable, though even on this point there is much diversity of opinion. But is this a correct standpoint from which to criticise Locke? We are not here dealing with a man who has chosen some literary topic in order to write brilliantly. An appreciation of the exigencies of the matter is necessary for an intelligent criticism and a fair estimate of the manner of such a work as the *Essay*. Locke's aim was not pure letters, but philosophical exposition. There is art for a purpose as well as art for art's sake; and written philosophy may be a contribution, and a very noble contribution, to literature, though it is far from being literature for literature's sake. We cannot blame the world if it makes the works of Locke immortal while it allows those of the man "who can write about Nothing like a "gentleman" to become obsolete.

But in appreciating our author it is also important to have in mind the literary characteristics of the period in which he lived. Locke's prose is the very embodiment of such an ideal medium as the spirit of the times led men to adopt. It was the age in which the modern scientific movement was beginning to tell upon the nation's life and thought. The whole intellectual atmosphere was changing as the result of the breezes of a freer and fresher knowledge. But while science flourished literature declined. This was due to the fact that the post-Restoration prose was transitional and was of importance chiefly for its reaction against the florid, disordered, high-flown manner of expression which had been the vice of the average prose of the age of Elizabeth and the Commonwealth. Compared with these epochs, the period marked by Locke is one of prosaic fact, being dominated by the fascination of a somewhat unromantic, unpoetical, scientific study of nature. Much of the prose of the time is a literal, commonplace retailing of matters of fact. Literature is very sensitive to the predominant spirit of the times and this is peculiarly the case with the post-Restoration writing. Nearly all the men of talent and learning who were a force in the intellectual life of England, literary men as well as scientific, poets as well as prose writers, were members of the then lately founded Royal Society. This institution had an important literary influence, and was a sufficiently near approach to the French Academy to set a certain fashion in English prose. Its action in the matter was not formal, but resulted from the fashion set by the literary standards adopted by its members. This reaction, led by the members of the Society, may be best appreciated by reading that section of Thos. Sprat's *History of the Royal Society* in which "Their Manner of Discourse" is described, and is spoken of as a not unimportant phase of their work and influence. " They have therefore been most rigorous in putting in execution, the " only Remedy, that can be found for this extravagance [in speech]: " and that has been, a constant Resolution to reject all amplifications, " digressions, and swellings of style : to return back to the primitive " purity, and shortness, when men deliver'd so many *things*, almost in " an equal number of *words*. They have exacted from all their members, " a close, naked, natural way of speaking ; positive expressions ; clear " senses ; a native easiness: bringing all things as near the Mathematical " plainness, as they can : and preferring the language of Artizans, " Countrymen, and Merchants, before that of Wits, or Scholars." [1] In no writer can this ideal prose of the Royal Society be better studied than in Locke. The *Essay* stands for the best that the typical member could do in the way of prose: while its shortcomings are those fostered by the very imperfect ideal which the scientific spirit created.

Let us endeavour to appreciate the qualities of the writings by which Locke has had so immense an influence on the development not only of English, but also of French and German speculation. As a philosopher, Locke may be described as a man of one book. His only other writings on the subject, besides the *Essay concerning Human Understanding*, are the three posthumous tracts written during his later life, *The Conduct of the Understanding, An Examination of P. Malebranche's opinion of seeing all things in God*, and *Remarks upon some of Mr. Norris's Books*. The first of these minor writings is really an unfinished chapter intended for the *Essay*. The second was also originally written as a chapter for the *Essay*, but friendliness towards

---

[1] *The History of the Royal Society*, by Thos. Sprat (1667), Pt. ii., Sec. xx.

Malebranche prevented him from publishing it. These posthumous writings are only of slight importance for our purpose. We are chiefly concerned with the *Essay*.

Locke himself was far from being satisfied with the form of the *Essay*. He tells us it was "written by incoherent parcels; and after "long intervals of neglect, resumed again, as my humour or occasions "permitted; and at last, in a retirement, where an attendance on my "health gave me leisure, it was brought into that order thou now "seest it. . . . The farther I went, the larger prospect I had: new "discoveries led me on, and so it grew insensibly to the bulk it now "appears in. I will not deny, but possibly it might be reduced to a "narrower compass than it is; and that some part of it might be "contracted; the way it has been writ in, by catches, and many "long intervals of interruption, being apt to cause some repeti-"tions."[1] It is certain that the order in which the topics presented themselves to the author's mind was very different from that in which they stand in the completed *Essay*. Locke appears to have first followed the natural train of his own thought, with its centre of interest in human knowledge. Having determined the possibilities and limits of knowledge, he then analysed the elements contained in actual experience. Lastly he reconstructed his materials, finishing where he at first began. This rearrangement in the reverse order in which he thought out the problems seems to have been determined by motives of logical sequence. It is probable that Book iv. was written first, and not last as its position in the *Essay* would suggest, then the main part of Book ii., then Book iii. and the remainder of Book ii., and last of all Book i. We get a truer conception of Locke's aim and of the historical development of his thought, if we begin reading the Fourth Book instead of the First. For there is a considerable change in the philosophical spirit from Book i. with its tinge of rationalism, to Book ii. with its simple introspection and decided empiricism. The discussion of Innate Principles at the commencement of the treatise is nothing like so effective as it would have been if it had followed the substance of Book iv.

Locke no doubt greatly improved the logical plan of the *Essay* by departing from the order in which he worked out the parts, but he lost considerably in organic unity and natural sequence. He was not careful enough with the literary reconstruction, and the plan has

---

[1] *Essay*, Epistle to the Reader.

become somewhat disorganised and dislocated. The bearing of the parts is not made manifest, and the exposition as a whole does not unfold in the facile manner that it might have done. It is apt to present itself as a mere string of detailed and detached analyses, interspersed with illustrations, maxims, and practical considerations. This may be avoided to a great extent by first getting the broader survey of the Fourth Book and entering into its spirit. The worst effect of writing "by incoherent parcels" is a diffuseness and repetition that is perhaps the most objectionable fault of the *Essay*. The modes of expression in which thoughts are reintroduced are not sufficiently varied. An old section is often re-inserted, with very little alteration, into a new context, where a mere reference or a gentle reminder would have sufficed. This desire for explicit logical completeness, we shall find, reappears in Locke's construction of sentences.

It might be thought that the highest possibilities of English prose as a philosophical medium had been exhausted in such styles as those of Bacon and Hobbes; but we find in the *Essay* a third distinct type, differing essentially from its predecessors, and possessing many new and excellent qualities for the exposition of abstract thought. The first and most characteristic quality of Locke's writing is the simplicity of his English. So far from writing in Latin, as Hobbes and Bacon had done to some extent, Locke used the most untechnical, idiomatic, and familiar English he could command. His powers of expressing abstract thought in such a medium are very great indeed, perhaps unequalled. To characterise briefly this most important quality of his prose, we need only repeat the description of the mode of expression adopted by the members of the Royal Society as "the language of Artizans, "Countrymen, and Merchants." It was with this instrument that he deliberately essayed to trace out the intricate labyrinths of knowledge. If in some degree he failed in precision, owing to this comparative roughness of his tools, the man of letters cannot, at any rate, complain of technicalities or a distrust of the mother tongue. The effect of this simple, homespun style, void of formalism and pedantry, has been very far-reaching. It consecrated the common speech of our country as the medium of our native abstract thought; it decided that England was to have a philosophical literature that could appeal to the nation and be brought into touch with the spirit of the times; and it hardly did less to determine what was to be the characteristic tone of English speculative thought than to set a model for its literary medium. In his choice of his native tongue as the sole vehicle of his thoughts to Englishmen, Locke completed that rupture with the past which neither Bacon nor Hobbes had the heart to make. Locke carried on with eagerness the polemic against bygone systems and their forms of expression. He was just the man to get rid of the last traces of pedantry and dead symbolism; and the times were peculiarly favourable, for not only was a more scientific, matter-of-fact treatment demanded, but the leaders of the literary movement were themselves carrying on a revolution against the swollen, intricate, and often bombastic prose of the past. Locke's masterpiece, so far as its language was concerned, could be read with ease by anyone who had even a small acquaintance with the literature of the day, and it needed no previous special training for an average intelligent Englishman to understand its arguments and follow its thought; for Locke's thoughts are as homespun as his style. He was never a great reader; he is the antipodes of an eclectic; and references to systems of philosophy are conspicuous by their absence. It was these features, together with its common-sense point of view, its ring of candour, and its practical bearings, that made the *Essay* so potent a factor in the intellectual life of England in the early Eighteenth Century. It was perused by a very miscellaneous class of readers, scientists, statesmen, gentlemen, men of the world, and religious people. It was not a book intended for the Schools, in whose quibbles and endless wranglings its author had no interest. It was a book for the nation, and the nation speedily made it its own.

Locke often writes against the false arts of rhetoric and the dangers of figurative modes of speaking. We should remember, however, that the period was in violent reaction against the obscurity, the long-windedness, and the high-pitched utterances so fashionable in the past. Hence Locke's remarks against the ornaments of language appear more extravagant to us who are not accustomed to those excesses of speech against which they were directed. Locke's style is not so devoid of figures and analogies as we should expect if we were to take his judgments on prose style quite literally. Still, the reaction, and Locke with it, went to the opposite extreme, even to the point of inelegance and baldness. But the movement did its work; for in Locke's prose there is no bombast, and very little ornament; of interminable sentences he has quite got rid, and extravagances of language are abolished. He puts his thoughts as clearly and intelligibly as possible; there is no attempt to give them importance by greatness of speech, or an appearance of depth by obscure utterance, or plausibility by the artifices of rhetoric. In order that we may vividly realise this style, we quote the following passage, in which dignity, and even stateliness, of tone is attained by simple words and easy sentences :—

"The infinitely wise Contriver of us, and all things about
"us, hath fitted our senses, faculties, and organs, to the con-
"veniences of life, and the business we have to do here. We are
"able, by our senses, to know and distinguish things; and to
"examine them so far, as to apply them to our uses, and several
"ways to accommodate the exigencies of this life. We have
"insight enough into their admirable contrivances, and wonderful
"effects, to admire and magnify the wisdom, power, and goodness
"of their Author. Such a knowledge as this, which is suited to
"our present condition, we want not faculties to attain. But it
"appears not that God intended we should have a perfect, clear,
"and adequate knowledge of them: that perhaps is not in the
"comprehension of any finite being. We are furnished with
"faculties (dull and weak as they are) to discover enough in the
"creatures, to lead us to the knowledge of the Creator, and the
"knowledge of our duty; and we are fitted well enough with
"abilities to provide for the conveniences of living: these are our
"business in this world. But were our senses altered, and made
"much quicker and acuter, the appearance and outward scheme of
"things would have quite another face to us; and I am apt to
"think, would be inconsistent with our being, or at least well-
"being, in this part of the universe which we inhabit."[1]

The following is the famous passage on "substance," and is very characteristic of Locke :—

"So that if anyone will examine himself concerning his notion
"of pure substance in general, he will find he has no other idea of
"it at all, but only a supposition of he knows not what support of
"such qualities, which are capable of producing simple ideas in
"us; which qualities are commonly called accidents. If any one
"should be asked, what is the subject wherein colour or weight
"inheres, he would have nothing to say, but the solid extended
"parts: and if he were demanded, what is it that solidity and
"extension adhere in, he would not be in a much better case than

---

[1] *Essay*, Bk. ii., Ch. xxiii., Sec. xii.

"the Indian before-mentioned, who saying that the world was
"supported by a great elephant, was asked, what the elephant
"rested on? To which his answer was, a great tortoise: but
"being again pressed to know what gave support to the broad-
"backed tortoise, replied, something, he knew not what."[1]

That this concession to the general reader was a real sacrifice of accuracy and precision is shewn by that fact that the great shortcoming of the *Essay*, as philosophical prose, is the lack of any adequate technical exactness in terms. Popular language and every-day idioms are used too exclusively to admit of unerring definiteness and unambiguity in the expression of subtle thought. There is a looseness and obscurity at most vital points of the exposition, arising from the employment of vague, common words, and the absence of technicalities. One instance, the most manifest and important, will suffice to shew this. The very core of Locke's system depends upon an examination of what he denotes by the general and indefinite term, the "idea." This word has to indicate, in turn, each of a jumble of most important psychological elements, which ought to have been distinguished by at least half-a-dozen technical terms precisely defined. The vague indefiniteness of the term is shewn by the definition which Locke gives at the outset,—Idea signifies "phantasm, notion, species, or what-
"ever it is, which the mind can be employed about in thinking."[2]
The following are some of the many widely different meanings in which the word is used:—

(a) Idea = sensation. "Concerning the simple ideas of sensation." *e.g.* "ideas of heat and cold, light and darkness, white and black,
"motion and rest." "Some faint ideas of hunger."

(b) Idea = feeling. "Though what I have here said may not perhaps
"make the ideas of pleasure and pain clearer to us than our own
"experience does."

(c) Idea = image. "The only way of retention is the power to
"revive again, in our minds those ideas which after imprinting have
"disappeared, or have been as it were laid aside out of sight; and this
"we use when we conceive heat or light, yellow or sweet, the object
"being removed."

(d) Idea = percept. "Our ideas being nothing but actual perceptions
"in the mind."

---

[1] *Essay*, Bk. ii., Ch. xxiii., Sec. ii.
[2] *Ibid.*, Intro., Sec. viii.

(e) Idea=concept. "Abstract ideas." "Substance" = "the idea "of we know not what support of such qualities which are capable of "producing simple ideas in us."

(f) Idea=imagination. "The idea of a centaur."

But apart from vagueness in the use of important terms, and looseness due to the attempt to replace philosophical nomenclature by untechnical modes of expression, Locke's vernacular is occasionally ambiguous simply through want of care in composition. The following sentence is a case in point. "There is nothing more evident, than that "the ideas of the persons children converse with (to instance in them "alone), are like the persons themselves, only particular." Here we have to gather from the succeeding sentence that what is meant by "the ideas of the persons children converse with" is, the ideas which children have of the persons they converse with.

Another weakness inherent in a style that adapts itself to popular modes of speech is the liability to lapse into a colloquial and too familiar manner of address. In many passages of the *Essay* we notice such a tendency, giving rise to a free and even careless air very different from the formality of Hobbes and the dignity of Bacon. Though many of these colloquial paragraphs are invaluable as easy methods of exposition yet, in places, it would be difficult to defend Locke against the charge of slovenliness. But this degeneration was the besetting sin of the prose of the period. Locke certainly never becomes common or coarse or vulgar as does so much of the contemporary literature. In this respect Hallam has justly said, "Locke is certainly a good writer, "relatively to the greater part of his contemporaries." When we have said our worst of the style of the *Essay* there is an engagingness in its native simplicity which endears it to the reader.

A second very important aspect of our author's writing is the types of sentence he adopts. Of these, there are, in the main, three, of which the syllogistic form, as it may be called, is the most striking. This kind of composition predominates in all the severer sections of the *Essay* and is quite a characteristic feature. Completeness and sequence of the clauses indicate the logical coherence and connection of the thought. This method of combining in the sentence, ground and consequence, premisses and conclusion, now first makes its appearance as a specific type in our philosophical prose. It is the result of Locke's extremely logical and undogmatic cast of mind. In the case of Bacon the secret of power lay in vividness of expression, brilliance of imagery,

D

gorgeous colouring of fancy, and glowing eloquence; in the case of Hobbes, in the sheer vigour and force of utterance. The peculiarity of Locke's prose, on the other hand, does not consist in the weight of the word, the force of the phrase, the artificial precision of statement, the fascination of ornament or the charm of rhetoric, but rather in the cunning logical web of the sentence as a whole. Each thread, in itself, is of little strength or beauty; it is the intimate structure of the written texture, woven out of unassuming, even unprepossessing words and clauses, that gives it durability and worth. Each complex sentence of this kind, is intended to stand or fall on its own merits. The effect of such a manner of writing is not cumulative, like that of eloquence; the author's aim is not to produce a general tone of feeling, but to lead us to certain definite propositions by the simple process of the logical syllogism. The ideal of such a type of construction of sentence is, that it should contain within itself the premisses of its own conclusion. To achieve this, there is a constant introduction of clauses with a present participle, giving the ground of the statement which follows in the body of the sentence. Hence also the very frequent use of the logical particles, " if," " since," " therefore," " thus," "for," " as," " because," "seeing "that," "so that." Perhaps this method of building the sentence is to be considered Scholastic in origin. If so, then Locke has not quite succeeded in freeing his exposition from the style of mediæval systems. It is certainly an important property of philosophical prose that the sentence should adapt itself easily to a strict syllogistic form. Few writers could be treated in this way better than Locke. The following quotations will illustrate the type of sentence we have been considering:—

" Since, therefore, whatsoever is the first eternal being, must
" necessarily be cogitative; and whatsoever is first of all things,
" must necessarily contain in it, and actually have, at least, all the
" perfections that can ever after exist: nor can it ever give to
" another any perfection that it hath not, either actually in itself,
" or at least in a higher degree: it necessarily follows that the first
" Eternal being cannot be matter. If therefore it be evident, that
" something necessarily must exist from eternity, it is also evident
" that that something must necessarily be a cogitative Being: for
" it is as impossible, that incogitative matter should produce a
" cogitative Being, as that nothing, or the negation of all being,
" should produce a positive being or matter." [1]

---

[1] *Essay*, Bk. iv., Ch. x., Secs. 10, 11.

"For certainty being but the perception of the agreement or dis-
"agreement of our ideas; and demonstration nothing but the per-
"ception of such agreement, by the intervention of other ideas, or
"mediums, our moral ideas, as well as mathematical, being
"archetypes themselves, and so adequate and complete ideas; all
"the agreement or disagreement which we shall find in them, will
"produce real knowledge, as well as in mathematical figures."[1]

There are some very ill effects of this manner of composition. It is too artificial to allow of a facile style. The mind is kept too taut, and is not allowed sufficient freedom. The order of the clauses is rarely the most natural, and the writing becomes over explicit and not sufficiently suggestive. It is this strictly logical style that makes Locke's prose in many parts intricate and laboured, in spite of the simplicity of the diction.

But the second type of sentence to which we would draw attention has even worse effects than the frequent use of those with a syllogistic framework. The latter, at any rate, attain logical sequence and unity, though it may be at considerable cost. But in many sentences qualifying clauses, modifying words, and complicating factors are introduced to such an extent and in such a haphazard, unpremeditated way, and the thoughts are allowed to straggle out in so disordered a fashion, that all structure and unity are lost. It is these sentences that hamper so much our author's prose, for they limp and hesitate in a most unpleasant fashion. The mind finds its way through the tangle with difficulty; we are no sooner started on a train of thought than we are pulled up by a distracting word or phrase, or our attention is dragged into a most unnatural direction. Such jerky, erratic, tortuous sentences enhance the pleasure we find in Locke's third manner of writing, namely, in smooth easy periods composed of short, natural, flexible sentences. This is the manner in which the major part of the *Essay* is written. Even subjects difficult of exposition are effectively treated in this truly modern English style. The sentences are not too complex, and not in the least stilted, and the natural order of the thought is aided by unaffected, unembarrassed fluency of expression. Contrast the following passages. The first will illustrate the dislocated, awkward sentence, lacking unity and structure; the second will represent Locke's facile natural style :—

"One may perceive how, by degrees, afterwards, ideas come

---

[1] *Essay*, Bk. iv., Ch. iv., Sec. vii.

"into their minds; and that they get no more, nor no other, than what experience, and the observation of things that come in their way, furnish them with, which might be enough to satisfy us that they are not original characters stamped on the mind."[1]

"The next thing to be considered is, how general words come to be made. For since all things that exist are only particulars, how come we by general terms, or where find we those general natures they are supposed to stand for. Words become general, by being made the signs of general ideas: and ideas become general, by separating them from the circumstances of time, and place, and any other ideas that may determine them to this or that particular existence. By this way of abstraction, they are made capable of representing more individuals than one; each of which having in it a conformity to that abstract idea, is (as we call it) of that sort."[2]

The third marked feature of our author's prose is its aptness in figure and illustration. The Essay abounds in various artifices whereby the subject may be made more concrete, and the exposition luminous and realistic. This is the secret of Locke's frequent employment of figures; and it is with reference to this manner of exposition that Hallam has said of Locke, what to most critics will appear strange, that "he is often too figurative for the subject." Figurative in the sense in which we apply that term to Bacon, Locke never is. In the *Essay* a figure is not for ornament, but for exposition; it is not the result of a prolific imagination, but of vivid conception. Locke's mind delighted in facts and experiments, in the concrete rather than in the abstract; hence his constant use of illustrations, examples, and analogies. Empirical philosophy, emphasising as it does the importance of the individual, particular facts of experience, lends itself peculiarly to the manner of illustrating doctrines that is so characteristic of Locke. To be quite strict, we should describe this feature of the prose of the *Essay* by saying that figures are plentiful while figurative language is rare. That is to say, a figure is generally introduced explicitly as such, and is not surreptitiously introduced into the language of the exposition. It does not seem that the figures Locke used led to any confusion there may be in his thinking, or to any obscurity in his writing. And if they are not true to fact, they are

---

[1] *Essay*, Bk. i., Ch. iv., Sec. ii.
[2] *Ibid.*, Bk. iii., Ch. iii., Sec. vi.

true, to a nicety, to his conception of fact, and indeed are often the means of our getting the most exact and clear notion of what his views really were. Every reader of Locke knows how important for the exposition are those adopted figures—the "tabula rasa" of the mind upon which ideas are stamped, and the impression of wax by the seal to represent the process of sensation—and that more original figure, "association" of ideas. These devices indicate most precisely the psychological doctrines of the *Essay*. We quote the following passage as interesting in this connection, since Locke was the first to use the expression "association of Ideas":—

"Besides this, there is another connection of ideas wholly "owing to chance or custom; ideas that in themselves are not all "of kin, come to be so united in some men's minds, that it is very "hard to separate them; they always keep in company, and the "one no sooner at any time comes into the understanding, but its "associate appears with it; and if they are more than two, which "are thus united, the whole gang, always inseparable, shew them- "selves together."[1]

Some of Locke's analogies are very quaint and ingenious, and shew considerable inventive power. The following is the realistic way in which he describes Malebranche's theory of seeing all things in God:—

"To conceive thus of the soul's intimate union with an infinite "being, and by that union receiving of ideas, leads one as "naturally into as gross thoughts, as a country maid would have "of an infinite butter-print, in which was engraven figures of all "sorts and sizes, the several parts whereof being, as there was "occasion, applied to her lump of butter, left on it the figure or "idea there was present need of."[2]

In speaking of the abuses of language, Locke uses a very apt analogy. He says that men who have no definite meaning for the words they use are "seldom to be convinced that they are in the "wrong; it being all one to go about to draw those men out of "their mistakes, who have no settled notions, as to dispossess a "vagrant of his habitation who has no settled abode."[3]

Occasionally we find Locke indulging in a more artistic and less

---

[1] *Essay*, Bk. ii., Ch. xxxiii., Sec. v.
[2] *An Examination of P. Malebranche's Opinion of seeing all things in God.* Sec. xix.
[3] *Essay*, Bk. iii., Ch. x., Sec. iv.

didactic use of figures. The following passage, from the *Conduct of the Understanding*, reveals him in his highest and happiest mood:—

> "It is not wise to play with error, and dress it up to ourselves or others in the shape of truth. . . . There are so many ways of fallacy, such arts of giving colours, appearances, and resemblances by this court dresser, the fancy, that he who is not wary to admit nothing but truth itself, very careful not to make his mind subservient to anything else, cannot but be caught. He that has a mind to believe, has half assented already; and he that by often arguing against his own sense, imposes falsehood on others, is not far from believing himself. This takes away the great distance there is betwixt truth and falsehood; it brings them almost together, and makes no great odds, in things that approach so near, which you take; and when things are brought to that pass, passion or interest, etc., easily and without being perceived, determine which shall be the right."[1]

But Locke is most adept at exemplification. The homeliness of his illustrations and examples matches his untechnical language and practical thought. They are drawn to a large extent from his knowledge of science and medicine, and are well adapted to his empirical doctrines. In expounding psychological truths, and making illusive mental facts vivid, Locke's powers are very great. Here there is full scope for examples; and these not only aid the exposition of abstract truths but also form the data upon which those abstract truths are based. He not only supplies abundance of examples, but the example is generally an organic part of the teaching. His interest in all branches of knowledge and all occupations of life, and especially his medical and scientific training, served him in good stead. The following is very typical of Locke's exemplification of great truths:—

> "Who perceives not, that a child certainly knows that a stranger is not its mother, that its sucking-bottle is not the rod, long before he knows that 'It is impossible for the same thing to be, and not to be.'"[2]

We are aware of the doctor and physiologist at every point of the *Essay*, and no department of knowledge could supply materials more useful for the point of view which Locke takes of the mind and its

---

[1] *Conduct of the Understanding*, Sec. xxxiii.
[2] *Essay*, Bk. iv., Ch. vii., Sec. ix.

functions. The following is an example given of the association of ideas :—

> "A friend of mine knew one perfectly cured of madness by a
> very harsh and offensive operation. The gentleman, who was
> thus recovered, with great sense of gratitude and acknowledge-
> ment, owned the cure all his life after, as the greatest obligation
> he could have received; but whatever gratitude and reason
> suggested to him, he could never bear the sight of the operator:
> that image brought back with it the idea of that agony which he
> suffered from his hands, which was too mighty and intolerable
> for him to endure."[1]

One illustration Locke is very fond of, is the operation for cataract.

> "If others love cataracts in their eyes, should that hinder me
> from couching of mine as soon as I can?"[2]

All sorts of scientific and commonplace facts are introduced to serve as instances and illustrations. This was entirely in harmony with the interests of the day, and shews us our author as a typical member of the Royal Society. The ploughman, dancing master, cobbler, opium, wax, gold, clocks, mirrors, centaurs, the loadstone, the microscopic appearance of sand and blood, etc., are introduced in the most offhand way, and some are repeated to such an extent as to become very stale. But all these things indicate what we ever feel in reading Locke, that breadth of view, that interest in all things human, and that candid open-mindedness which he so cultivated, and whose opposite he condemns in the following choice passage :—

> "They converse but with one sort of men, they read but one
> sort of books, they will not come in the hearing but of one sort
> of notions; the truth is, they canton out to themselves a little
> Goshen in the intellectual world, where light shines, and, as
> they conclude, day blesses them; but the rest of that vast
> expansion they gave up to night and darkness, and so avoid
> coming near it."[3]

It is rare for a man to be dominated by the scientific instinct and, at the same time, to be a literary genius; and certainly the weak side of Locke's character was the feebleness of his artistic imagination and æsthetic sense. There is no positive ugliness in his style; there are

---
[1] *Essay*, Bk. ii., Ch. xxxiii., Sec. xiv.
[2] *Conduct of the Understanding*, Sec. x.
[3] *Ibid.*, Sec. iii.

some natural graces; but Locke has not sufficient artistic interest to aim at any higher classic charm. From a literary point of view, it was an unfortunate age he represented; an age that spent its best energies in amassing facts rather than in creating masterpieces of literature or art. And Locke, though a thinker of great originality and penetration, was not gifted with constructive power to balance his analytical keenness. He was no system-builder, and was too easily satisfied with fragmentary and partial truth. He avoided ultimate issues, and his speculation was tethered by his common sense and prudence. His dislike of metaphysics, and his suspicion of over-subtleness in theory, prevented a thorough-going development of his principles to their legitimate conclusions. Hence the decidedly narrow scope of his doctrines. When Locke got to a certain point he refused to go beyond, though he could give no satisfactory reason as to why so far but no further. To the very end of the *Essay* we are conscious of the narrow limits prescribed by a practical, prosaic interest.

The possibilities of Locke's prose are very restricted owing to the narrow scope of the empiricism to which he confines himself. Empiricism is a theme for mediocre treatment; there is in it no room for high literary attainment either in structure or execution; there are not the impressive ideas that give the very soul to other philosophies. The *Essay* has none of the brilliance of a dazzling metaphysic, nor the elevation of a sublime ideal, nor the fascination of a restless striving after the ultimate bourne of knowledge and destiny, nor yet the solemnity that comes from a sense of the inscrutable unknown. Locke on some topics could be eloquent, but in his philosophy he had not a theme that could make him so.

The *Essay* is as faithful a reflection of the character and temperament of its author as any book in the language. Its simple, artless, homely style; its shrewd, practical deliverances; its modest unostentatious execution; its calm unheated argument; its scientific impartiality, catholic spirit and breadth of sympathy; its earnestness without dogmatism; its high-mindedness and dignity combined with humility and care; its avoidance of pedantry and all vanity and sham; its freedom from animus, party-feeling and all marks of a polemical and self-assertive disposition; its frankness, openness, and devotion to truth; all these qualities, for which the *Essay* is pre-eminently noted, are but the clear expression of the author's mind and temper.

IV.

George Berkeley.

To many minds George Berkeley is the most interesting figure in our native philosophy. Of this great man it would be difficult to say whether he is to be admired more for the untarnished beauty of his character, the subtlety of his speculation, or the charm of his literary style. All who knew him testified to the fascination of his personality; critics are equally unanimous and enthusiastic in their judgment that he is one of the classical writers of English prose. Berkeley's gifts were so many that, had they been divided, they would have made several great men. In him they are blended into a harmonious personality such as is the possession of very few. His literary talent causes him to stand out as no mean rival of our greatest prose authors; in imagination he is a poet, in brilliance of speculation he is unsurpassed. His enthusiasm made him an intellectual and moral force. When still a young man he published an account of one of the greatest psychological discoveries that has ever been made, and conceived that Idealistic philosophy which has done much to make dogmatic materialism an impossible creed for many minds,[1] while in later life he wrote the best modern representative of the Platonic dialogue.

Berkeley's position as a master of literary art needs no vindication; but it may be constantly referred to, seeing that, from the seemingly paradoxical nature of his doctrines, he is little known and little read. Himself loved by all, his works have been misunderstood by most, misinterpreted by many, read by few. Thus, although he is *the* philosophical classic in our mother tongue, not one of his writings became a household possession as did Locke's *Essay*. This is to a large extent due to the fact that Berkeley was not of the age in which he lived. We find him a man of enthusiasms amidst the frigid atmosphere of the early Eighteenth Century, an extreme Idealist amidst a frankly

---

[1] *E.g.*: Prof. Huxley writes thus of Berkeley's argument:—"I conceive that "this reasoning is irrefragable, and therefore, if I were obliged to choose between "absolute materialism and absolute idealism, I should feel compelled to accept the "latter alternative."—*Collected Essays*, Vol. VI., p. 279.

materialistic generation. Nor is he typical of even English thought, for, though Locke was his philosophical father, yet Berkeley is metaphysical as men rarely are who are native to British soil. Perhaps no one in modern times has reproduced the spirit and manner of Plato as did this Irish thinker. He possessed very extraordinary powers of metaphysical imagination, as we are soon made aware when we come uninitiated to his philosophy; for we find it needs considerable effort of imagination to follow him in his flights of Idealism. Dr. Johnson, through lack of this faculty, could never see the force or plausibility of Berkeley's arguments. But though the cast of our author's thought is all his own, his style has many features characteristic of the great literary epoch in which he lived. When he left Dublin and went to London he was soon recognised as one of the group of illustrious literary men chief among whom were Addison, Steele, Swift, and Pope. All his writings display those qualities of style which were cultivated to the utmost by the great essayists.

We not unfrequently hear insinuations to the effect that Berkeley's philosophical thinking and writing are vitiated by a religious bias; and John Stuart Mill has said, "The war against freethinkers was the "leading purpose of Berkeley's career as a philosopher." Such statements are apt to make unjust to Berkeley's pure, unbiassed speculative interest. His system is perfectly coherent and logical in itself apart altogether from any religious views he might possess. But the mind that conceived a system which reduced matter to the manifestations of spirit was sure to be a deeply religious one. Religion, however, could have nothing whatever to do with the psychological analysis which gave the cue to his whole system. His first two literary productions were manifestly the outcome of as pure a speculative motive as could possess any man. And, given the central conceptions of his philosophy as there set forth, given especially the doctrine of the immateriality of matter, it was impossible for him not to write against materialism. And since he found materialism at the root of the atheism and scepticism of the day, it was natural that he should wield his philosophical weapon against this prolific cause of irreligion. What we may justly say, therefore, as regards the motive of his writings, is, that Berkeley's fundamental conceptions are the outcome of a pure philosophical aim, that the bent of mind which explained the universe by a thoroughgoing spiritualistic theory could not be other than a deeply religious one, and that in his middle life he used the arguments framed against philosophical materialism to overthrow atheism and freethinking.

In nothing do we see more clearly the harmony of Berkeley's soul than in the relation of his psychology to his metaphysics, of his metaphysics to his religion, and of his religion to his life. This harmony of mind, heart, and life mirrors itself in his writings, and adds greatly to the unity of effect. It is the characteristic of his sentiments and style. Yet because of this complete unity, the beauty of our author's style is much more easily admired than analysed and described. His excellences as a writer are blended with such perfect taste and judgment, that the resulting effect does not force any all-predominating feature on the attention. This may be considered the perfection of writing, as of any fine art. Just as Hobbes is one of the earliest examples of uniform English, so Berkeley is one of the first instances of polished writing. Many authors surpass Berkeley in a few outstanding qualities, but in that balance and harmonious blending of various factors which brings us near perfection few are his equals. Some of the richness, imagery, and dignity of Bacon, he combines with the clearness of Hobbes and the natural freedom of Locke. But he has an advantage over his predecessors in that he lived in an age which produced the classical style of the great Essayists. The distinguishing qualities of the best prose of the period were just those with which Berkeley's style was most in sympathy. Yet even here our author may be said to have acquired all the virtues of classicism without developing any of its vices. For the intensity of his thought and the earnestness of his nature were sure safeguards against the formalism into which the fashion of the time was prone to degenerate. The chief excellences of our author's prose are vividness of conception, clearness of portrayal, and great range and felicity of expression ; a picturesque fancy, fertile imagination, with an earnestness ever and anon bursting into eloquence ; rhythm and flow of utterance, purity and elegance of diction, simplicity, directness, and lightness of speech. Berkeley indeed is one of the few men in whom artistic taste and reasoning capacity are equally developed. There is throughout his works a delicacy of imagination, of feeling and of language, an artistic sense of the beautiful as an element in the true, instinctively finding chaste and graceful expression, that makes Berkeley's fragments not only masterpieces of metaphysical subtlety but also most charming models of English prose. As a writer Berkeley is classical because he is dignified and correct, yet perfectly natural; earnest enough to impress, yet never blustering and uncontrolled; serious as becomes his subject, yet pleasing and vivid; polemical and vigorous, yet never bad-tempered or morose; imaginative and subtle, yet precise and luminous; using plain language but never descending to the trivial or commonplace.

Berkeley's philosophical works fall into three groups corresponding to the three periods of his literary activity. The first group contains those writings which set forth the speculations which engaged his attention while a student at Dublin, namely, *An Essay towards a New Theory of Vision* (1709), *A Treatise on the Principles of Human Knowledge* (1710), and the *Three Dialogues between Hylas and Philonous* (1713). The second period of authorship resulted in two works, published after his return from his missionary visit to Bermuda: *Alciphron, or the Minute Philosopher. In Seven Dialogues* (1732), and the *Vindication of the Theory of Visual Language* (1733). The third period, while he was Bishop of Cloyne, produced *Siris: A Chain of Philosophical Reflections* (1744).

There is considerable change in the style as it passes through these three periods, and this is especially noticeable on contrasting his first severer expositions with the more mature medium of later life. The characteristics of the first period of authorship are youthful ardour of manner, and persistent reiteration of, and logical argumentation around, his main contention. He writes as an isolated, original thinker who has evolved some fundamental truths, which he considers it of the utmost importance for mankind that they should be brought to perceive. The writings of the second period are polemical and popular in style; while his last work is marked by imaginative, mystical, poetical treatment in the form of aphorism, of more generous but less logical thoughts and with much enrichment from the sources of ancient philosophy.

The most important of Berkeley's writings for students of philosophy are the first two: *An Essay towards a New Theory of Vision* and *A Treatise concerning the Principles of Human Knowledge*, since these are the more severe expositions of his doctrines. The *Essay* is psychological in scope, analytical in method, and largely technical in manner. Rarely has a subject of this character—namely, the analysis of perception—been treated in so happy a way and with such literary attractiveness. There is much acumen and penetration in analysis, nicety and precision in the use of words, with grace of language and picturesqueness of detail. The style is logical, coherent, and clear. The very poverty of his technical terms drives him to simple description and vivid portrayal of mental facts. The following passage will indicate the easy and felicitous manner in which he unravels the tangle of the elements of perception :—

"From what we have shewn, it is a manifest consequence that the ideas of Space, Outness, and things placed at a distance are not strictly speaking, the object of sight; they are not otherwise perceived by the eye than by the ear. Sitting in my study I hear a coach drive along the street; I look through the casement and see it; I walk out and enter it. Thus, common speech would incline one to think I heard, saw and touched the same thing, to wit, the coach. It is nevertheless certain the ideas intromitted by each sense are widely different, and distinct from each other; but having been observed constantly to go together, they are spoken of as one and the same thing. By the variation of the noise, I perceive the different distances of the coach, and know that it approaches before I look out. Thus by the ear I perceive distance just after the same manner as I do by the eye." [1]

Apt and pleasing illustrations are part and parcel of Berkeley's writings :—

"The mind makes use of the greater or lesser confusedness of the appearance, thereby to determine the apparent place of an object. Nor doth it avail to say there is not any necessary connection between confused vision and distance great or small. For I ask any man what necessary connection he sees between the redness of a blush and shame? And yet no sooner shall he behold that colour to arise in the face of another but it brings into his mind the idea of that passion which hath been observed to accompany it." [2]

The *Essay*, however, is somewhat rambling and dislocated in treatment. It is restricted in scope, and the fundamental principles which naturally issue from Berkeley's psychological analysis are not propounded. Considered by itself, it lacks constructive grasp, and is engaged with details the import of which for the ultimate philosophy is not shewn. It has an independent value of its own, but is more properly to be looked upon as the first instalment towards the system

---

[1] *Essay*, Sec. 46. [2] *Ibid.*, Secs. 22, 23.

developed in his next work. It is a tentative effort—a preliminary
canter, so to speak—in which the author tries his powers.
In the *Principles*, we have Berkeley's central conception fully
developed and enthusiastically applied to the chief questions of knowledge. There is a more adequate constructive framework and better
proportion of parts, though, compared with such a work as Locke's
Essay, it is a feeble attempt at system. It is really an unfinished
work, Part II. never appearing, the manuscript having been lost.
But while there is a marked absence of artificial divisions and arrangement, for organic unity of treatment, essential coherence of thought,
and harmony in sentiment it is a model. From all possible points of
view, and with all available changes of expression and turns of
argument, the author emphasises and reiterates his great belief;
meeting all conceivable objections, anticipating all plausible ridicule,
examining all possible consequences, and removing all likely obstacles
to its acceptance ; arguing, coaxing, and manœuvring with all his
Irish wit and his fascinating manner until the result is almost
irresistible. The style is the perfection of felicity and grace. When
we commence to read the Introduction, we are at once charmed with
the rhythm and flow of language and the naturalness of manner.
Berkeley is as much at home in prose writing as a water-fowl in its
native element. The following passage will serve to illustrate his
simple, yet deft manner of expounding subtle thought and weaving
close argument :—

" I am content to put the whole upon this issue :—If you can
" conceive it possible for one extended moveable substance, or, in
" general, for any one idea, or anything like an idea, to exist
" otherwise than in a mind perceiving it, I shall readily give up
" the cause.

" But say you, surely there is nothing easier than for me to
" imagine trees, for instance, in a park, or books existing in a
" closet, and nobody to perceive them. I answer you may so,
" there is no difficulty in it; but what is all this, I beseech you,
" more than framing in *your* mind certain ideas which you call
" books and trees, and at the same time omitting to frame the
" idea of anyone that may perceive them ? But do not you your-
" self perceive or think of them all the while ? *This therefore is*
" *nothing to the purpose.*" [1]

---

[1] *Principles*, Secs. 22, 23.

There are passages also of great dignity and richness, some of them reminding us forcibly of Bacon, *e.g.*, *Principles*, 109. Occasionally there is scope for eloquence, and Berkeley never fails to rise to such an opportunity as occurs in the following wonderful passage:—

> "Some truths there are so near and obvious to the mind that a man need only open his eyes to see them. Such I take this important one to be, viz., that all the choir of heaven and furniture of earth, in a word all those bodies which compose the mighty frame of the world, have not any subsistence without a mind—that their *being* is to be *perceived or known*; that consequently so long as they are not actually perceived by me, or do not exist in my mind or that of any other created spirit, they must either have no existence at all, or else subsist in the mind of some Eternal Spirit—it being perfectly unintelligible, and involving all the absurdity of abstraction, to attribute to any single part of them an existence independent of a spirit." [1]

Passing over, for a moment, *Hylas and Philonous*, in order that we may consider all Berkeley's writings in dialogue together, we come to *The Theory of Vision or Visual Language Vindicated and Explained*, written after his return from Bermuda. It was published twenty-four years after the *Essay*, and is a reply to an anonymous letter which appeared in the Press, attacking his doctrine of Vision in eight observations. Berkeley's *Vindication* is thus necessarily polemical. In the first part of the tract, the objections are taken up one by one and refuted; in the second half, the doctrine is reconstructed synthetically as contrasted with the analytical procedure of the original *Essay*. The arguments are strong and forceful. The effect of polemic on his style is to make it firmer and more vigorous. But Berkeley is ever polished and polite, and his manner in polemic will be sufficiently indicated by the following extract:—

> "For my own part, if I were ever so willing, it is not on this occasion in my power to indulge myself in the honest satisfaction it would be frankly to give up a known error; a thing so much more right and reputable to denounce than to defend." [2]

Berkeley's *Dialogues* are something quite unique in modern philosophical literature. Others have written in dialogue, but none since Plato has embodied such cunning thought and speculative acumen in

---
[1] *Ibid.*, Sec. 6.   [2] *Vindication*, Sec. 32.

such excellent literary form, as Berkeley in his imagined conversations. He is the Plato of English, and indeed of modern philosophical literature. He is Platonic not only in conception and in tone, but also in style and treatment. By his *Hylas and Philonous* and *Alciphron* he may claim to be the modern master of the Platonic dialogue. Just as Plato used this form as the most suitable means of inculcating his doctrines and as the most powerful weapon against the scepticism of his day, so Berkeley adopted it, in his first dialogue, to explain his position, and, in his second, to carry on a polemic against the materialists, sceptics, and freethinkers of the Eighteenth Century. Though in no kind of prose is it more easy to write badly than in dialogue, Berkeley's written conversations are his most exquisite literary productions. In this form of writing he manifests considerable dramatic power, as also great variety and richness of thought, picturesque fancy and vivid expression, so that the elegance and fascination of these pieces can hardly be surpassed.

It was to free his doctrines from misunderstanding that Berkeley, in the person of Philonous, argued with an imaginary objector, Hylas. By the questions and replies of these three dialogues the author introduces his notions "into the mind in the most easy and familiar "manner." The work is a marvel of subtlety of thought and dexterity of argument, combined with general interest of treatment and great literary power. Having had the experience of the tentative effort of the *Essay* and having broached his central conceptions in the *Principles* he now has the advantage of seeing his doctrines in all their bearings, and in these dialogues, while the conversation moves quite naturally, there is better underlying system. Keen interest is maintained as Philonous is driven from first one position, then another, and is entangled in a complete web of argument. There is great clearness and perspicuity of language, and the style throughout is masculine and vigorous. Though the exposition is a popular one, all the leading thoughts get adequate explanation, and, having in mind both literary excellence and clear elucidation of his views, this dialogue is the best of Berkeley's works. Professor Fraser, who so fully appreciates Berkeley, says, "This work is the gem of British metaphysical "literature"; and further, "The clearness of thought and language, "the occasional colouring of fancy, and the glow of practical human "sympathy and earnestness that pervade the subtle reasonings by "which the fallacies of metaphysics are inexorably pursued through "these discussions, place the following *Dialogues* almost alone in the modern metaphysical library."

The annexed extract from the beginning of the *Third Dialogue* will shew the vigour and transparency of these artistic productions:—

"PHIL. What! say you we can know nothing, *Hylas*?

"HYL. There is not that single thing in the world whereof we can know the real nature, or what it really is in itself.

"PHIL. Will you tell me I do not really know what fire or water is?

"HYL. You may indeed know that fire appears hot, and water fluid; but this is no more than knowing what sensations are produced in your own mind, upon the application of fire and water to your organs of sense. Their internal constitution, their true and real nature, you are utterly in the dark as to *that*. . . .

"PHIL. But surely, *Hylas*, I can distinguish gold, for example, from iron: and how could this be, if I knew not what either truly was?

"HYL. Believe me, *Philonous*, you can only distinguish between your own ideas. . . .

"PHIL. It seems, then, we are altogether put off with the appearances of things, and those false ones too. The very meat I eat, and the cloth I wear have nothing in them like what I see and feel.

"HYL. Even so.

"PHIL. But is it not strange the whole world should be thus imposed on, and so foolish as to believe their senses? And yet I know not how it is, but men eat, and drink, and sleep, and perform all the offices of life, as comfortably and conveniently as if they really knew the things they are conversant about.

"HYL. They do so: but you know ordinary practice does not require a nicety of speculative knowledge. Hence the vulgar retain their mistakes, and for all that make a shift to bustle through the affairs of life. But philosophers know better things.

"PHIL. You mean, they know that they *know nothing*.

"HYL. That is the very top and perfection of human knowledge."[1]

There is a very fine passage in this same dialogue shewing Berkeley's poetical conception and choice language. We quote part of it:—

---
[1] *Hylas and Philonous.* Dialogue three. Works ed. by Fraser, Vol. I., pp. 322, 3.

"PHIL. Raise now your thoughts from this ball of earth to all
"those glorious luminaries that adorn the high arch of heaven.
"The motion and situation of the planets, are they not admirable
"for use and order? Were those (miscalled erratic) globes ever
"known to stray in their repeated journeys through the pathless
"void? Do they not measure areas round the sun ever propor-
"tioned to the times? So fixed, so immutable are the laws by
"which the unseen Author of nature actuates the universe. How
"vivid and radiant is the lustre of the fixed stars! How
"magnificent and rich that negligent profusion with which they
"appear to be scattered throughout the whole azure vault! Yet,
"if you take the telescope, it brings into your sight a new host of
"stars that escape the naked eye. Here they seem contiguous
"and minute, but to a nearer view immense orbs of light at
"various distances, far sunk in the abyss of space. Now you
"must call imagination to your aid. The feeble, narrow sense
"cannot descry innumerable worlds revolving round the central
"fires; and in those worlds the energy of an all-perfect Mind
"displayed in endless forms. But neither sense nor imagination
"are big enough to comprehend the boundless extent, with all its
"glittering furniture. Though the labouring mind exert and strain
"each power to its utmost reach, there still stands out 'ungrasped
"a surplusage immeasurable. Yet all the vast bodies that compose
"this mighty frame, how distant and remote soever, are by some
"secret mechanism, some Divine art and force, linked in mutual
"dependence and intercourse with each other, even with this
"earth, which was almost slipt from my thoughts and lost in the
"crowd of worlds."[1]

The second book of dialogues, *Alciphron, or the Minute Philosopher*, is the largest of Berkeley's works and of the most general interest and popularity. It is, however, far from being so strictly philosophical as his previous writings. It is mainly a theological and religious polemic with a philosophical groundwork. There are five persons in all, but only four enter into the conversation. The argument is freer and more desultory than in *Hylas*. The characters are more developed for dramatic purposes. It is richer in allusions to ancient thought, and there is more labour after artistic and rhetorical effect. Here and there occur sprightly passages and sallies of wit and touches of irony that are

---

[1] *Ibid.*, Dialogue two, Vol. I., pp. 302, 3.

perfectly Platonic. Professor Fraser says of these seven dialogues that they are "better fitted than any in our language to enable the English reader to realise the charm of Cicero and Plato." The following passages illustrate their picturesque setting and dramatic power:—

"This conversation lasted until a servant came to tell us the "tea was ready: upon which we walked in, and found Lysicles at "the tea-table. As soon as we sat down, I am glad, said "Alciphron, that I have here found my second, a fresh man to "maintain our common cause, which, I doubt, Lysicles will "think hath suffered by his absence.

"Lys. Why so?

"Alc. I have been drawn into some concessions you will "not like.

"Lys. Let me know what they are.

"Alc. Why, that there is such a thing as a God, and that His "existence is very certain.

"Lys. Bless me! How came you to entertain so wild a "notion?

"Alc. You know we profess to follow reason wherever it leads. "And in short I have been reasoned into it.

"Lys. Reasoned! You should say, amused with words, be- "wildered with sophistry."[1]

"Early the next morning, as I looked out of my window, I saw "Alciphron walking in the garden with all the signs of a man in "deep thought. Upon which I went down to him.

"Alciphron, said I, this early and profound meditation puts "me in no small fright.—How so? Because I should be sorry to "be convinced there was no God. The thought of anarchy in "nature is to me more shocking than in civil life: inasmuch as "natural concerns are more important than civil, and the basis of "all others.

"I grant, replied Alciphron, that some inconvenience may "possibly follow from disproving a God: but as to what you say "of fright and shocking, all this is nothing but mere prejudice. "Men frame an idea or chimera in their own minds, and then fall "down and worship it. Notions govern mankind: but of all "notions that of God's governing the world hath taken deepest "root and spread the farthest: it is therefore in philosophy an

---

[1] *Alciphron.* Dialogue four, Secs. 15, 16.

"heroical achievement to dispossess this imaginary monarch of
"his government. . . .
"My part, said I, shall be to stand by, as I have hitherto done,
"and take notes of all that passeth during this memorable event;
"while a minute philosopher, not six feet high, attempts to de-
"throne the monarch of the universe." [1]

The following passage from the same dialogue has great beauty of diction and rhythm :—

"ALCIPHRON. Perhaps I may not expect it, but I will tell you
"what sort of proof I would have: and that is, in short—such
"proof as every man of sense requires of a matter of fact, or the
"existence of any other particular thing. For instance, should a
"man ask why I believe there is a king of Great Britain? I might
"answer—Because I have seen him. Or a king of Spain? Because
"I had seen those who saw him. But as for this King of kings,
"I neither saw him myself, or anyone else that ever did see him.
"Surely if there be such a thing as God, it is very strange that He
"should leave Himself without a witness; that men should still
"dispute his being; and that there should be no one evident,
"sensible, plain proof of it, without recourse to philosophy or
"metaphysics." [2]

The following is a case of genuine Platonic irony :—

"ALCIPHRON. To speak my mind freely, this dissertation grows
"tedious, and runs into points too dry and minute for a gentle-
"man's attention."

In the *Siris*, Berkeley abandons formal exposition of his own peculiar views, and strings together much philosophical learning and the meditations of his later life, ingeniously calling them up in an examination of the medicinal properties of "tar-water." The parts of the book which are of philosophical interest are full of references to ancient systems, especially the Platonic, with which Berkeley had ever-increasing sympathy. It is thus of the nature of a mosaic-work, very cunningly fitted together, and abounding with many beautiful aphorisms and gems of thought; but with little of the logic, consistency, and precision of his youthful writing. The style is at times very similar to that of Bacon's *Novum Organum*; it is eloquent, learned, and polished, but without the naive simplicity or vigour of utterance which characterises Berkeley's early productions. As he became more

---

[1] *Alciphron.* Dialogue four, Sec. 1.   [2] *Ibid.*, Sec. 3, Dialogue four.

mystical in thought, his style mellowed correspondingly, and became more ethereal :—

"There is an instinct or tendency of the mind upwards, which
"sheweth a natural endeavour to recover and raise ourselves from
"our present sensual and low condition, into a state of light,
"order, and purity." [1]

He speaks thus poetically of "Phenomena":—

"The mind takes her first flight and spring, as it were, by
"resting her foot on these objects." [2]

The following are examples of the aphorisms of which *Siris* is largely composed :—

"As understanding perceiveth not, that is, doth not hear, or
"see, or feel, so sense knoweth not : and although the mind may
"use both sense and fancy, as means whereby to arrive at know-
"ledge, yet sense or soul, so far forth as sensitive, knoweth
"nothing." [1]

"Intellect enlightens, Love connects, and the Sovereign Good
"attracts all things." [3]

We will conclude our series of extracts with a typical passage from the *Siris* :—

"Human souls in this low situation, bordering on mere animal
"life, bear the weight and see through the dusk of a gross
"atmosphere, gathered from wrong judgments daily passed, false
"opinions daily learned, and early habits of an older date than
"either judgment or opinion. Through such a medium the
"sharpest eye cannot see clearly. And if by some extraordinary
"effort the mind should surmount this dusky region, and snatch
"a glimpse of pure light, she is soon drawn backwards, and
"depressed by the heaviness of the animal nature to which she is
"chained. And if again she chanceth, amidst the agitations of
"wild fancies and strong affections, to spring upwards, a second
"relapse speedily succeeds into this region of darkness and
"dreams." [4] . . . "The eye by long use comes to see even
"in the darkest cavern : and there is no subject so obscure but
"we may discern some glimpse of truth by long poring on it.
"Truth is the cry of all, but the game of a few. Certainly, where
"it is the chief passion, it doth not give way to vulgar cares and
"views ; nor is it content with a little ardour in the early time of

---

[1] *Siris*, Sec. 305. [2] *Ibid.*, Sec. 292. [3] *Ibid.*, Sec. 259. [4] *Ibid.*, Secs. 340, 1.

"life; active, perhaps, to pursue, but not so fit to weigh and revise. He that would make a real progress in knowledge must dedicate his age as well as youth, the later growth as well as first fruits, at the altar of Truth."[1]

One of the most admirable qualities of Berkeley's prose is the extent and richness of the vocabulary. As we traverse the smooth periods, we are allured by varied and picturesque words and kept on the alert by the dexterity and happiness of phrase. But with all his powers of expression and great gifts of language, Berkeley is often vague and loose in places where he ought to be strict, owing to the fact that he has not an adequate fixed nomenclature. This defect was much less disastrous in Berkeley's case than in Locke's, for, excepting his psychological analysis of perception, his doctrines could dispense with an elaborate equipment of terms better than most philosophies. As a Nominalist, Berkeley denied the real existence of abstract ideas. The effect of this on his exposition was to keep the thought, for the most part, in the region of the concrete. Consequently, the exposition takes on a descriptive manner as opposed to the style which is little more than a manipulation of abstract terms. Our author's fondness for the concrete, and his vivid description of psychological and metaphysical truths, make his writings suggestive and interesting as contrasted with the arid waste of abstractions and tiresome tangle of argument which form so large a part of many philosophies. Moreover, Berkeley was instinctively poetical, and the concrete with him usually means the picturesque. His genius as a writer lies in the direction in which Plato excelled, in impregnating simple language with subtle metaphysical import.

Berkeley has no very elaborate or complicated arguments to construct, and his thought moves unhalting in a single line, straight for its goal. We are led as quickly and as immediately as possible from sense-experience to the ultimate nature of existence. Perhaps no thinker has taken so short a cut to his main contention, or returned to it so persistently. And when his central conception is once vividly realized, it leaves an impression that is indelible. Berkeley is no system-builder; his treatment is somewhat slight. His works were not wrought out as a laboriously constructed edifice, but were the result of some most brilliant strokes of genius. But though his doctrines did not stand in need of an elaborate expository system, yet

---

[1] *Ibid.*, Sec. 368.

they were most admirable subjects for treatment in what are perhaps best called philosophical fragments. Thus, while saying all he has to say in a manner most natural and effective, he comes nearer, in subject-matter and treatment, to the ideal literary topic than most who handle abstruse subjects.

But though slight in system and simple in manner, it is remarkable how quickly Berkeley penetrates to the farthest recesses of metaphysics. He is no trifler, no mere ingenious man with a fad; nor is he a vain visionary. It is his grasp of ultimate issues that makes him clear and earnest. What lack there is of the imposingness and strength of an elaborate structure, he makes up for by the impressiveness of intensity and zeal. His speculative, humanist, and religious interest centred on his one great doctrine, and produced an enthusiasm and glow that, allied with his powers of artistic imagination and expression, could not but result in noble literature. For Berkeley not only maintained the greatest earnestness of manner, he was also gifted with more poetic feeling, fine sentiment, and artistic taste than any of our native philosophers. Hume and Berkeley alone exhibit the ease and grace of the French metaphysicians. Berkeley possessed a vividness of conception and a liveliness of imagination that made his views of the world almost as realistic to him as the ordinary view is to most people. This vivid Idealism gave, especially to his later works, great scope for delicate, imaginative writing. The doctrines of the "divine visual language," the "immateriality of matter," "sense symbolism," "*esse est percipi*," etc., could only be expounded in a style very different from that suited to the mechanical theories of Hobbes or the common-sense views of Locke.

It was Berkeley's theme that did more than anything else to make him a great writer. He conceived a philosophy into the advocacy of which he could throw his entire earnest nature. To find a more whole-hearted, ardent soul were impossible; and throughout life he had a single theme, one that never lost, for him, its truth or fascination. Every question he brings to the touchstone of his great conception. *That* remains worthy of his subtle intellect and persistent advocacy. Of *that* he never wearies; in it he never loses faith; its truth is ever coming to his mind in a fresh vision. It is the inspiration of this, his all-absorbing principle, that makes him one of the greatest advocates to whom the world has ever listened. His highest aim in life was to make men realize the truth, self-evident to him, that real activity cannot attach to dead matter, and that *things* are but the *sense-symbols* of spirit. That men take the symbols for the substance, and turn what are merely states of consciousness into an unthinking, independent something, matter,—this was the delusion Berkeley conceived to have taken possession of men's minds, and from this he strenuously endeavoured to free them by all his ingenuity of thought and skill of exposition. It matters not (since we are considering the question of style only) whether we think Berkeley's theory entirely true, partially true, or utterly false; but it is much to the point, that to its originator it was the verity of verities, and that, animated by it, he produced literature of the highest type. Berkeley attained a mastery of the noblest prose, largely because he was so entirely in the hands of a great theme. We venture to think that no English philosopher has had a theory of the universe upon which he could so entirely concentrate his whole being, and to the propagation of which he could bring faculties so varied as those of Berkeley; a philosophy whose very simplicity is its beauty, and yet which utilized the combined powers of subtle analysis, poetic fancy, lofty sentiment, and fervid advocacy. How different a theme, in respect of capacity, from those restricted ones of Locke and Mill! How inspiring and ennobling as compared with the Materialism of Hobbes, the Scepticism of Hume, or the Agnosticism of Spencer! We do not wish it to be supposed that we pit the beauty of art, or the grandeur of eloquence, against the truth of logic or the strength of reason. But the history of literature shews that the men who have attained the highest art have been those with the noblest themes. Many theories of the universe and of the nature of man have taken away everything of the deepest and most sublime import, and have desecrated the ideals, the beauty, and the poetry of the world. They may be true, but it is surprising if beauty and truth are so utterly incongruous, and if that which most deserves acceptance by the minds of men should, by a strange irony of fate, be denied the arts which have ever proved most able to perpetuate ideas. If the fittest in art is alone to survive, then we had better betake ourselves, not to theories that of necessity restrict themselves to the quibbles of argument, the snarls of cynicism and the negations of doubt, but to such as create a literature that charms by beauty, ennobles by ideals, and persuades by eloquence. When men can find in materialism or uncertainty themes as inspiring as Berkeley's Idealism, then, and not till then, may they be found to write as he.

V.

David Hume.

DAVID HUME has come down to us, not only as the metaphysician of the Eighteenth Century who brought about a revolution in speculative thought, but also as the brilliant historian and man of letters. It has been truly acknowledged that literary ambition was the mainspring of his life. He, of all our native philosophers, aimed most consciously and deliberately at literary renown, and we naturally expect the writings of such a man to afford an excellent study in style. He is the type of an abstract thinker and a polished writer combined; for he is one of the few greatest thinkers at whom the literary historian and critic does not shrug his shoulders and pass by on the other side. This enviable reputation, as literature, which Hume's philosophical works have attained, may be due, to some extent, to the reflected glory they have caught from their author's brilliance as a historian and essayist. By what other means they have acquired the praise that has been bestowed upon them we shall be able to consider.

Hume's first, and juvenile work, *A Treatise of Human Nature*, now regarded as one of the world's philosophical possessions, met with by no means such a reception as satisfied its author's thirst for fame. He expected that the principles of the *Treatise* would turn the world upside down, and his mortification was great when he found its advent did not even " excite a murmur among the zealots." It was to remedy the defects of this work, which were indicated by its lack of popularity, and which Hume considered to lie more in the " manner " than in the " matter," that he adopted what may be regarded as his second philosophical style in re-casting his doctrines into the form in which we find them in the *Enquiry concerning Human Understanding* and the *Enquiry concerning the Principles of Morals*.

Hume's literary merit in the sphere of philosophy is invariably judged by the undoubted excellence of the *Enquiries*. The estimate that he is "the master of philosophic English," and that he is "unsurpassed in mastery of philosophic style," is due entirely to the literary form of the *Enquiries*, and especially of the *Enquiry concerning the Principles of Morals*. Of the latter work Hume said, "In my own "opinion (who ought not to judge on that subject), it is, of all my "writings, historical, philosophical, or literary, incomparably the best." Hume's second style, as shewn in the *Enquiries*, is undoubtedly of greatly superior literary value to that of the Three Books of the *Treatise*. Whether he could have re-written the whole of the *Treatise* in his later style without impairing the philosophy, we cannot say, though it is very questionable. The point we have to notice is, that though, in comparison with the *Treatise*, the literary qualities of the *Enquiry* have been vastly improved, its philosophical value has simultaneously deteriorated to an even greater degree, so much so, that most authorities have come to the conclusion that it would be an injury to philosophy, as well as an injustice to Hume himself, to regard the wish of his old age, which Mr. Grose characterises as "the posthumous "utterance of a splenetic invalid," that the *Enquiries* "may alone be "regarded as containing his philosophical sentiments and principles."

It is unfortunate for our estimate of Hume's philosophical style that the *Enquiry* is not his masterpiece, that it far from adequately sets forth his philosophical views, that his position as a thinker among the world's thinkers could not be maintained on its merits, and, lastly, that its superiority as literature was attained by very questionable means. We are thus in a difficulty with regard to Hume's styles. If we take the *Enquiries* as our criterion, then his prose is not here pre-eminently his philosophical prose : if on the other hand we base our judgment on the *Treatise*, which is his great philosophical work, his prose is of a different and of a much inferior quality. Philosophers, looking at his *Treatise*, say that Hume is one of the greatest thinkers : critics, with an eye to his *Enquiry concerning Morals*, declare that he is the most admirable English philosophical writer. When Hume raises his literary standard, he at the same time lowers his philosophical standard. We can only get a correct estimate of his literary worth, therefore, by keeping in mind the relation, philosophical and literary, between the *Treatise* and the *Enquiry*.

The *Treatise* is difficult and tiresome, whereas the *Enquiry*, by which Hume wished his earlier work to be entirely superseded, is a comparatively easy and pleasant book. How was this change in general literary interest and worth achieved? Certain it is that Hume added nothing of importance to his philosophical position as propounded in the *Treatise*. Its lack of success in the world was one of the chief causes of his abandoning speculation and turning to other more popular and productive spheres. The *Enquiry*, therefore, had nothing to gain from new truths bearing on his system. Any important additions were of another character and were made for the sake of gaining popularity and effect. The same motives influenced him in excluding from his later book philosophical questions of the most vital importance to his doctrines. Many radical changes, however, in the manner and treatment of the *Enquiries* are great improvements, and indeed result in quite a different philosophical style.

To shew how impossible it is to take our estimate of Hume's style from the *Enquiry* alone, as also to indicate by what means he increased its literary worth, we will notice firstly its additions, secondly its omissions, and thirdly its change in treatment and tone.

(1) Broadly speaking, the additions are two topics of a non-philosophical character. Section x., "Of Miracles," and Section xi., "Of a particular providence and of a future state," are quite new, and were evidently introduced to give zest to a work written in the Eighteenth Century, and from the desire "to excite a murmur among the zealots" which had been frustrated by the cool reception of the *Treatise*. That this is the case, and that they are not legitimate developments of his philosophy, is clear from the fact that the argument against miracles is quite inconsistent with Hume's fundamental denial of any necessary connection in causation. The sections are exceedingly interesting and lively, and contain some of his best writing; but the motive for their introduction is sufficiently manifest, and along with many other indications goes to support the opinion that Hume was "often both more " and less than a philosopher."

(2) The omissions are also instructive from their literary aspect. The whole of the 2nd Part of the 1st Book of the *Treatise*, on the abstruse and vexed subject, "Of the ideas of space and time," is omitted in the *Enquiry*. This wholesale exclusion of nearly one quarter of the corresponding part of the *Treatise* is fatal to the worth of the *Enquiry* as an exposition of Hume's doctrines. It is an illustration of the way in which Hume was prepared to sacrifice some of his most fundamental views on philosophy, and those without which

his other doctrines could not be supported, simply because he had failed to treat them in a manner acceptable and palatable to the general reader. Part iv. of the *Treatise* is dealt with in very similar fashion, being inadequately represented in Section xii. of the *Enquiry concerning Human Understanding*. The important discussion of the question of "abstract ideas" is in the *Enquiry* relegated to a short note. These three facts alone are sufficient to destroy the importance of the *Enquiry* as a philosophical classic, when compared with the *Treatise*. Book ii. of the *Treatise*, which contained the somewhat dry, but all-important psychological mechanism of the "passions and will," and was thus organically related to the *Morals*, appeared with only small verbal improvements as the separate and thus useless work, the *Dissertation on the Passions*. The consideration of "Liberty and Necessity," its most important section, had already been transferred to the *Enquiry* as a likely companion to "Miracles." In sum, the psychological groundwork is cut out as dry and incompatible with literary quality, difficult and harassing problems are shirked, and the solid structure of the system most seriously damaged. But though the general interest of the work is greatly increased, and the call upon intellect and attention adapted to the ordinary reader, the perusal of the *Enquiry* is in one important sense far more unsatisfactory than the perusal of the *Treatise*. We feel that something of radical importance has been removed, and the doctrines are left hanging in the air. Hume sold his philosophical birthright for a mess of pottage.

(3) When Hume has thus introduced topics capable of freer treatment, and avoided troublesome and hard details, he succeeds in completely transforming the literary dress. The whole treatment and style of the *Enquiries* is agreeable and graceful as compared with the work of his youth. The *Enquiry concerning Morals* especially, presents quite an inviting appearance.

One of the most marked improvements is the change of tone. The pugnacious, arrogant, dogmatic air is greatly modified. He does not irritate us so constantly by challenging contradiction. There is not so much disregard for the sentiments and sympathies of mankind, nor such cavilling, captious handling of instinctive beliefs. Further, his sceptical and isolated position, though sufficiently manifest even here, is not so constantly forced on the attention. His attitude is more conciliatory; paradoxes are not so strikingly stated; inconsistencies in reason and life are not so heartlessly exposed; his principles are not so ruthlessly forced to unpleasant conclusions. Though the *Enquiry* loses a great deal of the interesting personal element of the *Treatise*, it gains by being most decidedly less egotistic. The following is a comparison of extracts from corresponding passages of the two books. The passages are substantially the same, but the alteration from the egotistic style of the *Treatise* to the impersonal, general statement of the *Enquiry* is not only an indication of increased literary modesty, but is a great improvement in philosophical expression :—

Treatise, Book ii., Pt. iii., Sec. ii.	*Enquiry concerning Human Understanding*, Sec. viii., Pt. ii.
"I define necessity two "ways."	"Necessity may be defined "two ways."
"I place it either in . . . ."	"It consists either in . . ."
"The only particular in "which anyone can differ from "me, is . . ."	"The only particular in "which anyone can differ, is, " " ."
"I may be mistaken in as-"serting, that we have no idea "of any other connection in the "actions of body, and shall be "glad to be further instructed "on that head: But sure I am, "I ascribe nothing . . ."	"We may here be mistaken "in asserting that there is no "idea of any other necessity or "connection in the actions of "body: But surely we ascribe "nothing . . ."
"Let no one, therefore, put "an invidious construction on "my words, by saying simply, "that I assert . ."	(Deleted.)
"I change therefore no-"thing."	"We change no circum-"stance."

The self-assurance of the youth who is just beginning to feel his own powers is most painfully manifest on every page of the *Treatise*, and Hume lived to repent its "positive" temper. The earlier book however has a personal style, and therefore a fascination, which is not retained by the later one. It shews us Hume as a solitary thinker at

La Flèche working his way through the maze of problems amidst which he found himself. Though not, in form, so personal as the *Method* and *Meditations* of Descartes, yet the tone is very similar. We feel as we follow the almost feverish pen that wrote the *Treatise* that we are really dealing with the biography of its author's personal thought. The individuality of Hume, with its idiosyncrasies, is stamped on every thought and expression. This personal style is, for the most part, lost in the *Enquiry*. Hume had in the meantime come to look at those same problems and his own peculiar solutions of them with the less romantic and, at the same time, less earnest gaze of his later vision. He has in the *Enquiry* lost the ardour of his first love for Philosophy, and he transcribes his thoughts in a more impersonal and a less impetuous style.

The *Enquiry*, on the other hand, certainly gains inasmuch as the matter retained for treatment is not so unwieldy, and the crop of problems not so thick as to cause confusion. The *Treatise* is not characterised by well-proportioned, systematic exposition. It is often rambling and diffuse. It lacks unity of plan and arrangement, though the natural cohering power of the thought is great. The texture as a whole is loose and knotty. So many threads are started, and woven in after so irregular a fashion, that the design is often confused by the crossing, recrossing, and twisting of the strands of thought and argument. The *Treatise* casts about its wealth in littered confusion. As exposition, the book lacks judgment. The author fights many a side issue in a way that might lead us to think a central position is being attacked, while often an insignificant outpost becomes the key to a future situation. But the style of the *Treatise*, though in many respects embarrassing to the reader, yet delights to such an extent in variety of statement and reiteration of truth that it is, spite of its disorder, very striking and effective composition. In the *Enquiry*, on the other hand, Hume aims more at a single line of consecutive thought with all the attendant advantages of facile movement. But while we have got rid of confusing detail, we have also lost our foundations, and the logical system of the *Treatise* is hopelessly mutilated. The *Enquiry* gained greatly as exposition, we will not say *by* the sacrifice of, but still, along with the sacrifice of, logical coherence and stability. We cannot say that the *Enquiry* arouses that keen curiosity which the *Treatise* is well calculated to inspire. The course the author's thought takes him in the latter book is a free and easy speculative ramble. We are never quite sure where he is going next. He turns all sorts of corners and brings us out in many surprising situations. The whole work indeed is the very opposite of a cut and dried, formal exposition of doctrines.

Turning to Hume's style in the narrower sense, we find the diction of the two works is of very different value. The characteristic qualities of the *Treatise* are directness, flexibility, and force; those of the *Enquiries* flowing ease, balance, and grace. The manner of the *Treatise* is one of great freedom and vigour; the language is not uniformly precise, while at times there is a struggle for utterance and the subtle thought is ill-expressed. All this is in marked contrast with the fluency and elegance of the maturer style. The movement of the prose of the *Treatise* is quick, restless, and at times, random. The sentences are short and broken, and have the appearance of coming ready to hand with little premeditation and less afterthought. They approximate to the truth, and indicate it, rather than clearly and strictly define it. The language is simple, untechnical, every-day English, used with a freedom that approaches the colloquial, a directness that is almost abrupt, and at times with a slovenly reiteration that is tedious and annoying. Perhaps the most pleasing feature of the style of the *Treatise* is the fresh, naive way in which it describes its truths. Hume has a very graphic manner of portraying mental facts. He is always simple, unconventional and vivid, at times quaint and curious, and very often picturesque. The following quotations will illustrate this aspect of the style of the *Treatise*:—

"'Tis evident at first sight, that the ideas of the memory are much more lively and strong than those of the imagination, and that the former faculty paints its objects in more distinct colours, than any which are employ'd by the latter. When we remember any past event, the idea of it flows in upon the mind in a forcible manner; whereas in the imagination the perception is faint and languid, and cannot without difficulty be preserv'd by the mind steddy and uniform for any considerable time."[1]

"The mind is a kind of theatre, where several perceptions successively make their appearance; pass, re-pass, glide away, and mingle in an infinite variety of postures and situations. There is properly no *simplicity* in it at one time, nor *identity* in different; whatever natural propension we may have to imagine

---

[1] *Treatise*, Bk. i., Pt. i., Sec. iii.

"that simplicity and identity. The comparison of the theatre
"must not mislead us. They are the successive perceptions only,
"that constitute the mind; nor have we the most distant notion
"of the place, where these scenes are represented, or of the
"materials, of which it is compos'd." [1]

In homely unrestrained freedom of style the *Treatise* has marked affinity with Locke's *Essay*, to which however it is superior in force and dexterity of expression and in vivacity of manner. It is, on the other hand, inferior when considered from the side of systematic exposition; one very great source of confusion being the postponement of the treatment of "impressions" to that of "ideas." The genuineness and modesty of Locke's style are markedly absent from Hume's writing, and at times we think we catch an insincerity of tone. Our author's superior vigour and piquant smartness were in some degree due to French influence. The *Treatise* was written during his seclusion in France, and Dr. Johnson said of this, Hume's first work,—"In "style . . . so far as the structure of sentences is concerned, no "doubt he was already influenced by the literature of France."

When we turn to Hume's second style, we pass from choppy, disordered composition to smooth periodic writing. The *Enquiry* is easy in treatment, lucid in statement, regular and elegant in style. This, Hume's more mature manner, required the less technical and less subtle topics of the *Enquiry concerning the Principles of Morals* for it to be seen at its best. There is throughout the *Enquiries* a very real increase in precision and exactness of expression. The sentences are more luminous and more carefully constructed. Much of the looseness of the earlier work has disappeared. Elegance, flow, and grace are attained chiefly by the balance of the sentence, and the poising of groups of words. But the literary artifices are so constantly and uniformly employed that they become very manifest "knacks." The sentences are the work of a practised hand, and the diction reminds us of Plutarch, and shews his influence. Much of the force and naturalness of the early manner is exchanged for this regularity and polish. The resulting impression is that of artificial monotony. There is no natural, unconventional grace, and no spontaneous elevation. Throughout the beauties are restricted to the regular, austere, classic type. At his best, Hume does not write with the unaffected grace of Berkeley; nor can it be said of him, as it may truly be said of Bacon, that he is

---

[1] *Ibid.*, Bk. i., Pt. iv., Sec. vi.

inspiring and inspired. The following passage is typical of the philosophical style of the *Enquiries* :—

"All men, it is allowed, are equally desirous of happiness, but few are successful in the pursuit: One considerable cause is the want of strength of mind, which might enable them to resist the temptation of present ease or pleasure, and carry them forward in the search of more distant profit and enjoyment. . . . And however poets may employ their wit and eloquence, in celebrating present pleasure, and rejecting all distant views to fame, health, or fortune; it is obvious, that this practice is the source of all dissoluteness and disorder, repentance and misery. A man of strong and determined temper adheres tenaciously to his general resolutions, and is neither seduced by the allurements of pleasure, nor terrified by the menaces of pain; but keeps still in view those distant pursuits by which he, at once, ensures his happiness and his honour."[1]

The *Enquiry concerning the Principles of Morals* has gained in wealth of illustration, and in references to History and past thought. The examples and analogies of the *Treatise* are introduced for the elucidation of difficult discussions, and for a figurative representation of abstruse views ; in the *Enquiry*, Hume finds them a means of enlivening and enriching his pages. The illustrations of the *Treatise*, indeed, serve as philosophical experiments, and are a very important part of the ingenious means Hume adopts " to introduce the experimental Method of Reasoning into Moral Subjects." Hence they are somewhat technical in character, being manufactured to prove and illustrate a definite doctrine. The following contains one of these ingenious illustrations constructed by our author to exemplify his theory of Abstract Ideas :—

" 'Tis certain that the mind wou'd never have dream'd of distinguishing a figure from the body figur'd, as being in reality neither distinguishable, nor different, nor separable ; did it not observe, that even in this simplicity there might be contain'd many different resemblances and relations. Thus when a globe of white marble is presented, we receive only the impression of a white colour dispos'd in a certain form, nor are we able to separate and distinguish the colour from the form. But observing afterwards a globe of black marble and a cube of white, and

---

[1] *Enquiry concerning the Principles of Morals*, Sec. vi., Pt. I.

"comparing them with our former object, we find two separate
"resemblances, in what formerly seem'd, and really is, perfectly
"inseparable. .... When we wou'd consider only the
"figure of the globe of white marble, we form in reality an idea
"both of the figure and colour, but tacitly carry our eye to its
"resemblance with the globe of black marble: And in the same
"manner, when we wou'd consider its colour only, we turn our
"view to its resemblance with the cube of white marble."[1]

Hume's illustrations are chosen and manipulated with the greatest judgment, and, just like those of Locke, are a very intimate part of the exposition. The following, which occurs in both the *Treatise* and the *Enquiry*, is a very effective argument on the question of the "freedom
" of the will ":—

"A prisoner, who has neither money nor interest, discovers
" the impossibility of his escape, as well from the obstinacy of the
" gaoler, as from the walls and bars with which he is surrounded;
" and in all attempts for his freedom chuses rather to work upon
" the stone and iron of the one, than upon the inflexible nature of
" the other. The same prisoner, when conducted to the scaffold,
" foresees his death as certainly from the constancy and fidelity of
" his guards as from the operation of the ax or wheel. His mind
" runs along a certain train of ideas: The refusal of the soldiers
" to consent to his escape, the action of the executioner; the
" separation of the head and body; bleeding, convulsive motions,
" and death. Here is a connected chain of natural causes and
" voluntary actions; but the mind feels no difference betwixt
" them in passing from one link to another."[2]

The following is worth mentioning as an instance of very striking illustration. It exactly represents Hume's position on the question of "necessary connection."

"If we reason *a priori*, anything may appear able to produce
" anything. The falling of a pebble may, for ought we know,
" extinguish the sun; or the wish of a man control the planets in
" their orbits."[3]

The *Treatise* is peculiarly lacking in references to either ancient or modern systems; it is written in the isolated style which refuses to

---

[1] *Treatise*, Bk. i., Pt. i., Sec. vii.

[2] *Ibid.*, Bk. ii., Pt. iii., Sec. i.

[3] *Enquiry concerning Human Understanding*, Sec. xii., Part iii.

draw directly on the past, or to ally itself with the feeling and sentiment with which the past is linked. It is throughout the product of a solitary thinker, working indeed with the thoughts of the past, but using them as the intellectual atmosphere of the world, and therefore as common property. The philosophical style most opposed to this is to be found in the *Lectures* of Sir William Hamilton, whose pages are as full of references to philosophers, renowned and obscure, as the *Treatise* is free from them.

There is in many of Hume's statements an obscurity which defies penetration, a woefully inadequate stock of philosophical terms, and an inexactness and looseness in the use of those he does possess almost as great as in the case of Locke. Exchanging Locke's term "idea" for "perception" to denote all mental phenomena, Hume sets out with a strict distinction between "ideas" and "impressions." In a note to one of the early pages of the *Treatise* he writes, "I here make use of "these terms, *impression and idea*, in a sense different from what is "usual, and I hope this liberty will be allowed me. Perhaps I rather "restore the word, idea, to its original sense, from which Mr. *Locke* "had perverted it, in making it stand for all our perceptions." Beyond this improvement by the limitation of the term "idea," Hume's philosophical nomenclature and stock of psychological technicalities is as poverty-stricken and inadequate as that of other native writers previous to the time of Sir William Hamilton.

We now come to the question of Hume's relative merit as a philosophical writer. Mr. Grose has so highly estimated Hume's position as to make him "the one master of philosophic English." If by "philosophic English," we mean a cold, passionless language which is incapable of the highest and noblest qualities of literature, this estimate of the style of the *Enquiries* is perhaps just. But if "philosophic" comprehends all the properties of writing that may with good effect be employed for the exposition of philosophical thought, there is one writer who might be preferred to Hume as possessing far superior qualities to even those exhibited in the *Enquiry concerning Morals*. From a comparison of Hume's works with Berkeley's, without any reference to the nature of the thought expressed, and merely with style as the criterion, we would not hesitate to say that Berkeley is by far the greater writer.

If we compare Berkeley's philosophical masterpiece with that of Hume (and they were both written when their authors were at about the same early age), we find that it is more fascinating in manner and equally effective in style, that it is far more luminous, and greatly superior in elegance and elevation. If we compare the best passages of Berkeley with the best of Hume there can be no doubt of the former's surpassing beauty and eloquence. It might be objected perhaps that Hume's subject-matter is more typically philosophical, and no doubt Berkeley's writings gain something by being fragments, though it is remarkable how many of Hume's positions are anticipated therein and how coherent a system may be extracted from them. But apart from the fact that all Berkeley's work is as philosophical in nature as Hume's *Enquiry concerning Morals*, we fortunately have considerable psychological analysis in Berkeley's early works, and can thus compare his powers with Hume's severest and strictest philosophical style.

Compare for instance Berkeley's discussion of "Abstract Ideas" in Secs. 6–25 of the *Introduction* to the *Principles of Human Knowledge*, with Hume's examination of the very same question in Sec. vii., Pt. i., Bk. i., of the *Treatise*. After characterising Berkeley's view as "one of "the greatest and most valuable discoveries that has been made of late "years in the republic of letters," Hume goes on to support it from exactly the same position, by essentially similar psychological analysis and argument. Thus the conditions and restrictions of the subject, as well as the age of the writers and the nearness of the times of writing, render a comparison of styles legitimate. And we think it unquestionable that, though perhaps for ingenuity and elaborateness of argument Hume is superior, and for striking exposition, felicity of illustration, force and flexibility of language, he cannot well be surpassed, yet for precision and lucidity of style Berkeley is superior; while in natural grace and flow of diction, in elegance of manner, and in unity of effect, he shews himself pre-eminent as a literary genius.

Hume was typical of English thought in the Eighteenth Century, just as Bacon was entirely characteristic of the Elizabethan Age. The cold, keen, critical spirit of the time found its representative in David Hume. We must not expect therefore to find in his writings the fervour, the grandeur, or the imagination of a past era. Berkeley's unique position in English philosophical prose is due to the fact that he was not exclusively of either age, but possessed the spirit of the old, with the powers of thought and expression of the new.

Hume has two disqualifications for attaining the highest literary excellence as a speculative writer. The one arises from the limitations of a prosaic character, the other from his unfortunate position in the historical development of thought. Hume was intellectually intense; yet it was a cold, keen, critical intensity, rather than that which results from fervour and enthusiasm. His character was peculiarly devoid of qualities of an heroic and lofty cast. His mental constitution is defective through absence of the finer sentiments, æsthetic tastes and emotional feeling. These limitations were fatal to the highest attainment in literature of any class, not excepting even philosophy. He is vivid in conception, facile in expression, buoyant and energetic in temperament; but his feelings are remarkable neither for depth, power, nor loftiness. The restricted range of his tastes prevented him from becoming a great literary artist; his emotional feebleness rendered it impossible for his writings ever to become powerful as a direct social force; while his lack of appreciation of, and reverence for, the ideal, excluded his philosophical works from the number of the greatest masterpieces of literature.

It is often declared of Hume that he is destitute of imagination. If by this we mean constructive imagination the statement is just, and indicates a very radical defect of our author's mind, and one which greatly limited the scope of his work. With metaphysical imagination of a certain reach Hume was endowed in a remarkable degree. But while it was such as to enable him to free himself of the ordinary conventional mode of regarding experience and to divest his mind of every trace of the common-sense associations of thought, it always stopped short at this negative, divesting stage, and never went on to positive construction of a philosophical interpretation of the world. To say that Hume was destitute of imagination would render it impossible to explain the thorough-going, uncompromising scepticism of his thought; while on the other hand the fact that he stopped short at scepticism is accounted for by his deficiency of imagination of a constructive character. What imagination he did possess gave a fanciful, curious tone to much of his writing and added greatly to its fascination; but there is a total absence of that constructive power which can alone create great literary masterpieces.

Such qualities of character and temperament, however suited for the production of a psychologist, were bound to result in defects of style and treatment. Hume never warms to anything except sarcasm, and the lack of the artistic faculty is only too manifest. Though he has acquired an artificial dignity and elegance, it can never be said of him, as it may be said of Berkeley, that he is one of the most charming of all writers of English prose.

Secondly, Hume's peculiar position in the development of thought, and the destructive, sceptical tendencies of his mind, whereby he made a climax in that development, would not admit of those qualities of style necessary for the highest place in literature. Whatever Hume himself was, and however much or little he staked on his philosophy, that philosophy is in tone utterly sceptical, its aim is philosophical nihilism, and its result paralysis in the realm of thought and reason. We have shewn that the crude materialism of Hobbes was not a theme to be handled with the greatest literary success. It is no less certain that the scepticism of Hume was sufficient in itself to paralyse the finest powers of prose writing. The only message that Hume has for men is the contradictory one that no message is possible. His whole attitude of thought is negation, his last word on every subject the "everlasting no." Such a philosophy was bound to acquire peculiar properties of style; but those qualities could not be the highest of which philosophical prose is capable. The fact of Hume's position being what it is, and his literary medium being restricted to the explanation of that position, excluded some of the noblest qualities from Hume's writings. We are not hereby making any reflection on the thought; we are merely indicating the necessary and legitimate influence of the thought on the expression.

The literary superiority of the *Enquiry concerning the Principles of Morals* is, to some extent, due to the advance Hume there makes beyond his usual sceptical position. Again, in reading the group of philosophical Essays, *The Stoic, The Epicurean, The Platonist,* and *The Sceptic*, in which he personates the respective types of philosophers (as Milton does two of them, in the form of verse, in *L'Allegro* and *Il Penseroso*), we are struck by the remarkable change in style, when we pass from the first three Essays to the last. In *The Stoic, The Epicurean,* and *The Platonist,* which constitute the most popular part of all Hume's philosophical writings, he quite surpasses himself in splendour of language and in fervour of utterance. This is evidently the result of his throwing himself, heart and soul, into the decided characters he is personating and the positive doctrines he is, for the moment, upholding. It is the inspiration of the subject that effects this temporary change in Hume's style. Though much too florid and high-flown, it is significant that Hume acquires more power in the assumed *rôle* of an inspiring character than in the exposition of his own doctrines. When he puts on *The Sceptic* in the fourth of this group of Essays, he descends to a style suitable to the tone of thought, and more in keeping with his usual manner.

The mental state of the writer of the *Treatise* is vividly and touchingly depicted in the following passages, which occur in the concluding section of the First Book :—

"Methinks I am like a man, who having struck on many "shoals, and having narrowly escap'd ship-wreck in passing a "small frith, has yet the temerity to put out to sea in the same "leaky weather-beaten vessel, and even carries his ambition so "far as to think of compassing the globe under these disad-"vantageous circumstances. My memory of past errors and "perplexities makes me diffident for the future. The wretched "condition, weakness, and disorder of the faculties, I must employ "in my enquiries, increase my apprehensions. And the im-"possibility of amending or correcting these faculties, reduces "me almost to despair, and makes me resolve to perish on the "barren rock, on which I am at present, rather than venture "myself upon that boundless ocean, which runs out into im-"mensity. This sudden view of my danger strikes me with "melancholy: . . . I am first affrighted and confounded "with that forlorn solitude, in which I am plac'd in my philo-"sophy, and fancy myself some strange uncouth monster, who, "not being able to mingle and unite in society, has been expell'd "all human commerce, and left utterly abandon'd and discon-"solate. Fain wou'd I run into the crowd for shelter and "warmth; but cannot prevail with myself to mix with such "deformity. I call upon others to join me, in order to make a "company apart; but no one will hearken to me."

Further on he thus sums up the sceptical results of the First Book of the *Treatise* :—

"We have, therefore, no choice left but betwixt a false reason "and none at all. For my part, I know not what ought to be done "in the present case. . . . The *intense* view of these manifold "contradictions and imperfections in human reason has so "wrought upon me, and heated my brain, that I am ready to "reject all belief and reasoning, and can look upon no opinion "even as more probable or likely than another. . . . Most

"fortunately it happens, that since reason is incapable of dis-
"pelling these clouds, nature herself suffices to that purpose. . . .
"I dine, I play a game of back-gammon, I converse, and am
"merry with my friends; and when after three or four hours'
"amusement, I wou'd return to these speculations, they appear so
"cold, and strain'd, and ridiculous that I cannot find in my heart
"to enter into them any farther. . . . If I must be a fool, as
"all those who reason or believe anything *certainly* are, my follies
"shall at least be natural and agreeable."

Hume seems to have been only too glad to relax his ardour in such speculations. Most men would have found life simply intolerable on such an intellectual basis; few men could have brought themselves to write philosophy in such moods. But though Hume argues with his whole, keen, penetrating intellect, he never advocates with his whole soul. Perhaps, indeed, Hume's definition of a soul as a "stream" or "series" of impressions and ideas is a truer description of his own, than of most men's. There were not in him the powerful emotional forces which weld a man's being into an undivided whole. Few if any have been found so ready to commit philosophical suicide; and probably no great thinker's doctrines have influenced his own life so little as Hume's affected his. For he could close his *Treatise* and forget the annihilation of reason that had been there committed, and he could live the very enjoyable life of a man who had never vexed his mind with speculation. Such has not been, and could not be, the way with men of the noblest character. It has been well admitted that Hume lived two lives, the life of a sceptical thinker, and the life of an ordinary jovial Scotchman with a weakness for applause; and the remark has often been made that the two were not by any means harmonious, even if they were compatible. They did not appear incompatible to Hume, but they would have been to a greater and a more genuine philosopher.

Our author's philosophical works lack those ideal and constructive elements which are so essential to great literary undertakings. There is the absence of some of the highest moral qualities, of the elevation and greatness of tone, which philosophy is so pre-eminently calculated to inspire. On the moral questions where Kant thrills us by the magnificence and nobility of his conception and the surpassing dignity of his periods, Hume is decidedly mediocre. We are not aware of a single instance in his speculative works of true loftiness and grandeur of sentiment or expression. The doctrine of absolute, final doubt, may and indeed must, be expounded in very direct and forcible terms ; but it cannot use the gentler or the nobler arts. It utterly fails to inspire confidence or assume the attitude of advocacy or persuasion. Its whole manner is depressing, and more calculated to give rise to insincerity and trifling, to melancholy and sarcasm, than to play upon the imagination, wake the chords of eloquence, or echo the thunders of sublimity.

VI.

John Stuart Mill.

JOHN STUART MILL was the most popular and influential English philosophical writer in the second and third quarters of the Nineteenth Century. This ascendancy was due, no doubt, chiefly to the sympathy of his thought with the tendencies of the times, and partly also to the personality of Mill, but in no small degree to the popularity of his style. To understand Mill, whether as a thinker, a man, or a writer, needs very careful study. For he has been a perplexing puzzle to the students who have tried to reconcile his philosophical tenets, and to the biographers who have done their utmost to analyse his character and do justice to his life. His literary style also presents itself as a puzzle; for there is throughout his writings a reserve of manner which leads us to suspect that self-revelation is not to be looked for here to the same extent as in the case of ordinary writers. Yet this restraint, which is so uniform a mark of our philosopher's prose, is itself an inevitable indication of character. Style never really belies the mental qualities of which it is the outcome. And when we consider how difficult it was for Mill's real self to struggle into life, is it surprising that he has not revealed his inmost nature in his style? It may be questioned whether the real John Stuart Mill ever did live; such had been the effect of the force employed to imprint the mould of other minds upon his. When we consider his highly-strung temperament and keen sensibility, the extraordinary educational processes through which his father put him, the eccentric influences to which he was early subjected, and the subsequent expansions of his character and sentiment, is it any wonder the world cannot be said to know the real John Mill? He hardly knew himself.

Mill's preposterous early training, together with his sensitiveness to outside influences, effectually prevented the growth of a very strongly marked individuality of style. We do not find his prose by any means so characteristic as that of previous great philosophical writers. His style is not a simple one; nor in the strict sense is it a compound: it is a mixture. Thus, though we have chosen it as a type, it is typical of a mixed style possessing many qualities which it contains rather than blends. An impressible nature, an openness to the many-sidedness of truth, was the striking characteristic of Mill's mental constitution. The play of manifold forces upon so finely sensitive a mind greatly influenced his thought, and through his thought, his style. But in very different ways; for while it destroyed the coherence of his doctrines, it saved his style. This impressionableness made his mind receptive to many views which his acknowledged principles would not of themselves have led him to adopt. He was instinctively aware of the elements of truth in widely divergent and even opposed schools of thought. Hence the practical working principle he adopts in all his philosophising is to take the middle course between extremes. The verdict of later thought upon Mill appears to be, that though he tried hard to conciliate, he has not succeeded in harmonising. For we find his philosophy a mixture of very miscellaneous ingredients. In Metaphysics, Logic, and Ethics, he performs some very remarkable feats in mixing elements that refuse to mingle. Because of this, there is great difficulty in saying precisely to what philosophical school Mill really belongs. This receptivity of mind brought him under the influence of many philosophies. Comte and Wordsworth appealed to him no less than Bentham. Hartley, James Mill, Berkeley, Kant, Coleridge, and German Idealists, all supplied ingredients for his mixture. What Mill does is little more than to glue together the bits he has selected, and smear over the joining. Thinkers regret that his susceptibility to the many-sidedness of truth was not supported by a sufficiently constructive power of mind. Readers who study Mill's style are grateful that the author is constantly passing out of one atmosphere of thought and sentiment into another. Mill's powers of language were so inferior to those of the great masters who had preceded him that, unless his mind had been a sensitive, and his philosophy a chequered one, he would not have succeeded as a popular and interesting writer. What powers of expression he did possess he cultivated to the utmost; but his natural gifts in this respect were so ordinary as to preclude the possibility of his ever becoming a great master in literature. Moreover, these limited powers of expression were stunted in early life by perhaps the most absurd education ever forced upon the mind of a child. Mill's literary productions never shewed that spontaneousness and vigour of style which he might, under more favourable circumstances, have developed. That his manner was not rendered hopelessly pedantic was due to his responsiveness to more generous influences, and to his intense practical interests. These latter, indeed, were an invaluable counteraction to the deadening influence of a forced education and of much speculative thought. Absorbing practical objects and great public spirit are the key to Mill's life, as they were the inspiration of his work. He was by nature an abstract, analytical thinker, with very limited literary gifts. Nothing could save such a man from utter failure in the world of letters unless the power of very practical motives for writing. Mill at any rate owed it to his father that he was, from the outset of life, inspired by very noble yet tangible objects to labour for. James Mill was no seventh-heaven speculator ; neither was Bentham ; and there could hardly be a school of philosophic thought with more definite aims and greater scope for propagandism than that in which Mill may be said to have been born and bred. His early surroundings and youthful precocity soon had the very natural effect of leading him to regard himself as a quite superior individual, destined to be of some importance as a reformer of the nation's thought and a destroyer of the popular prejudices. And though experience modified his youthful ambitions, Mill's thought was throughout life influenced by a practical interest which, even in his most abstract moods, he never quite outsoars. For his practical aims were ever of a kind falling in with, or rather issuing from, his speculations. And the more practical his motives, the more powerful his writings. It has been said that our author had no interest in the concrete for itself, and that he could never therefore become a poet. This is very true. Mill is never even picturesque; but at any rate he is practical; and though artistic expression did not attach to his thoughts, yet practical interests issue very naturally from his doctrines ; and such practical interests, if they do not inspire poetry, can at least animate prose.

The works in which we may study Mill's philosophical style are the *System of Logic*, *Utilitarianism*, *Examination of Sir William Hamilton's Philosophy*, and *Auguste Comte and Positivism*. We might also add the philosophical portions of the *Dissertations and Discussions* and the three posthumous essays on *Nature, The Utility of Religion*, and *Theism*. The *Principles of Political Economy* deals with a subject which we relegate to the special sciences. The tracts *On Liberty* and *On Representative Government* are chiefly of political interest, while the *Autobiography* is purely personal. Mill's works could not by any colouring of enthusiasm be made to appear fascinating. What we may say is, that they are very readable for the average mind. They will certainly not live and be read, like the works of Bacon, Berkeley, and Hobbes, simply in virtue of their style. But though not marked by any great beauties of literary finish, or enriched by artistic execution, Mill's writings were very widely read, and were deservedly popular as possessing some of the more sober excellences of philosophical prose.

We have said that Mill's style presents very varied features. These we shall be able to appreciate by looking at our author in three different aspects; first, as an abstract scientific expositor; secondly, as a popular persuasive advocate; thirdly, as an able dialectician.

Mill's aim, of taking the elements of truth contained in divergent theories and embodying them in his own doctrines, had a very marked effect on his exposition, in that his powers of systematic and orderly discourse were called forth to a far greater extent than if he had been carried away by an overmastering idea or by a one-sided view of things. He builds his philosophy, it does not grow. Where unity does not result from inherent vitality of thought, it has to be acquired by plan and system. It is in the region of what has been termed the middle ground of thought that Mill, as a thinker, is most at home and most successful; and it is here that the art of exposition can be best applied. The author of the *System of Logic* is a master of that comparatively modern acquirement, the art of orderly, systematic treatment of the text-book type, the absence of which is so great a drawback to the productions of earlier philosophers. He shews great skill in planning and arranging his subject-matter, and rare power in enunciating principles, and in knitting together a body of doctrines. His formulation of the branch of Logic in which his great worth lies, namely, the Inductive Methods of the Sciences, is, considered as exposition, masterly. The experimental methods are reduced to the fewest and simplest forms, and the five Canons are enunciated with exactitude and precision.[1] Each method is expounded, its workings explained, its limits and values remarked. Then follows exact scientific exemplification of the several types of procedure. We have only to compare this orderly unfolding and due elaboration of thought with

---

[1] There has been much adverse criticism of Mill's Methods, and improved formulations of the Canons have been suggested; but these are really questions of Logic, with which we have no concern.

Bacon's *Novum Organum* to realize what a change has come over our art of exposition. Indeed, the difference in this respect even between Mill and Hume is remarkable, and is probably to be accounted for largely by the influence of the formal manner of Sir William Hamilton. One of the best pieces of exposition Mill ever did, is to be found in his two articles entitled *Auguste Comte and Positivism*. He was deeply influenced by the Positivist philosophy, and his account, in this article, of its chief exponent's views leaves little to be desired. The system is unfolded in a single thread of consecutive thought, and we are given an insight into the main tenets with the maximum of ease and in a very short space. Usually the sentences contain a thought of sufficient body without undue complexity, though occasionally we come upon a straggling style of composition, whereby, for the sake of brevity, thought is tacked on to thought in the same sentence. The language in this article on Comte is remarkably clear and precise, and there are many faultless sentences and paragraphs. Other excellent and very interesting pieces of exposition are found in those chapters in the *Examination of Sir William Hamilton's Philosophy* in which Mill sets forth his own views on the important questions of the existence of the external world and of the mind, and in which he discusses the question of the freedom of the will.

The abstract, formal style of our author is somewhat lacking in force and point because of its very perfection as well ordered, philosophical statement. He is indeed a most conventional writer, never shocking us by any eccentricity of manner. No real literary genius could have written in so colourless and impersonal a way as that in which Mill constructs his abstract sentences. No doubt his forms of expression are far more available for ordinary writers than any our philosophical masters had employed. Average mortals could not copy to advantage these characteristic and inimitable styles. There is in Mill's works an entire absence of that indefinable, personal element which renders the style of great writers unique. There are hardly any idiosyncrasies of expression, and few signs of restless, quickening life. His passages are lucid and sustained without any mysterious influence or inexplicable effect. It is such as an ordinary educated mind, of an abstract and unimaginative cast, would naturally adopt wherewith to express its thoughts. It is ordinary pedestrian prose.

Mill's diction is marked by a calculated precision amounting to what, with a less weighty manner, would be primness, and by a lucidity at times the less apparent because of the density of the vocabulary employed. Mill's efforts as a composer were almost entirely taken up with the laborious endeavour to get his thoughts clearly expressed. It is difficult to imagine writing clearer and with less of superfluity than Mill's strictly philosophical prose. He does not wrap his thoughts in cloudy effusions; every idea has the appearance of being crystallised with clean cut edges and sharply defined angles. Indeed the formality of Mill's abstract prose is such as to produce an apparent precision of style that is not always the result of precision of thought. The following short passage will illustrate the easy intelligibility and the definiteness of Mill's writing:—

"Logic, however, is not the same thing with knowledge, though the field of logic is coextensive with the field of knowledge. Logic is the common judge and arbiter of all particular investigations. It does not undertake to find evidence, but to determine whether it has been found. Logic neither observes, nor invents, nor discovers; but judges." [1]

Along with these admirable qualities, and to a great extent nullifying their effect, we find certain sombre and unattractive features. Judging merely from our author's diction we should have little difficulty in concluding that the writer, whoever he might be, must have lived since Dr. Johnson influenced English prose. Many of the most potent forces of Mill's life were calculated to produce an affected and pedantic mode of expression. He had a strong liking for sonorous words and phrases and almost invariably prefers a long word to a short one. As a result his style is often pompous and not infrequently the sound is greater than the thought. Mill's vocabulary is often ponderous, his phrases unwieldy and his sentences long. Many of his sentences indeed are regular verbal bombardments. The following quotations will indicate his swollen style:—

"The claim assumes that character of absoluteness, that apparent infinity, and incommensurability with all other considerations, which constitute the distinction between the feeling of right and wrong and that of ordinary expediency and inexpediency." [2]

"We are continually informed that Utility is an uncertain standard, which every different person interprets differently, and that there is no safety but in the immutable, inefface-

---

[1] *System of Logic*, Vol. I., p. 9.   [2] *Utilitarianism*, p. 81.

"able, and unmistakeable dictates of Justice, which carry their evidence in themselves, and are independent of the fluctuations of opinion."[1]

This ponderousness of diction in the more serious exposition has a deadening influence. Had Mill written uniformly in this heavy, laborious manner, there would have been no demand for People's Editions. The meaning is quite clear indeed if we read carefully; he knows exactly what he wants to say, and says it without abnormal complexity of statement and with great precision; and yet the ponderousness of his diction and the weight of his phrases oppress us. The reader is conscious that these periods are equal to any occasion, however imposing, and that they could convey any matter, however weighty. We feel there is great work on hand, and that so authoritative and dignified a bearing must needs be the accompaniment of powerful thought and momentous undertakings. There is no lightness, no rapid movement about Mill's sentences. They lack vigour and impetus. They are slow, deliberate, and massive. The manner is eminently sane and sober. Hurry and excitement are undignified; speed is out of the question where there is such mass; enthusiasm is unscientific.

Contrast with Mill as he has hitherto appeared to us, namely, as an abstract, cold, heavy, scientific writer, with a precise but somewhat dreary style, Mill, the persuasive advocate and the plausible, popular writer. Mill's supreme object—the propagation of certain truths and the overthrow of certain prejudices—would not allow him to write merely as an abstract speculator, who would be rarely read. Nor, as we have indicated, was he a philosopher likely to tumble into the well while contemplating the stars. He always had an eye on each, or rather, he kept glancing from one to the other. This frequent return to earth, if we may so speak, did much to ruin the consistency of his philosophy, and at the same time to save his style. For while it would not allow him to follow out his original principles when they developed into paradoxes and unpleasant practical issues, it constantly brought him down from abstruse statements to a popular, descriptive style. Thus, though from his education and forced habits of thought he was infected with ponderosity and dullness, as a result of his many-sided interests and his devotion to great practical ends, Mill constantly reverts to a plain-spoken, easy, and untechnical manner. The

---

[1] *Ibid.*, p. 82.

Utilitarianism shows us this popular style at its best. Here our author is for the most part homely and simple, and there is a sustained intensity and an effective advocacy not to be found in his larger works. Here and there we come upon passages which, by their simplicity and purity, remind us of Plato. The following quotations, the second of which has become quite a classical passage, will illustrate these properties of style :—

"Questions of ultimate ends are not amenable to direct proof. Whatever can be proved to be good, must be so by being shown to be a means to something admitted to be good without proof. The medical art is proved to be good, by its conducing to health; but how is it possible to prove that health is good? The art of music is good, for the reason, among others, that it produces pleasure; but what proof is it possible to give that pleasure is good."[1]

"It is indisputable that the being whose capacities of enjoyment are low, has the greatest chance of having them fully satisfied; and a highly-endowed being will always feel that any happiness which he can look for, as the world is constituted, is imperfect. But he can learn to bear its imperfections, if they are at all bearable; and they will not make him envy the being who is indeed unconscious of the imperfections, but only because he feels not at all the good which those imperfections qualify. It is better to be a human being dissatisfied than a pig satisfied; better to be Socrates dissatisfied than a fool satisfied. And if the fool, or the pig, is of a different opinion, it is because they only know their side of the question. The other party to the comparison knows both sides."[2]

Though Mill's dignity sometimes deteriorates into stiffness, his homeliness never becomes vulgarity. His prose, when he is in the mood, can come sufficiently near to the tone of conversation and can put itself in touch with the reader's interest and difficulties without becoming colloquial or desultory. Mill ever retains the measured style seemly for a writer, and never appears in undress though he is often familiar and pleasing.

An element contributing greatly to the popularity and effectiveness of Mill's prose is its use of illustrations. His materials are derived mainly from the facts and theories of science and from his knowledge

---

[1] *Utilitarianism*, p. 6.   [2] *Ibid.*, pp. 13, 14.

of practical affairs. There are no spontaneous creations of imagination; his examples have a didactic worth and give a literary relief, but do little more. Mill never makes his statement *in* a figure, though he may render an abstract discussion concrete by example or analogy. His scientific illustrations were, as he tells us, obtained second hand. To them the most interesting chapters of the Logic, *e.g.*, those in the Book on Fallacies, owe much of their charm. But Mill not only exemplifies in this way, he frequently insinuates a principle into the mind by an apt illustration or a homely analogy. It may be the instance of the "village matron" to typify induction from particular to particular; or the case of the miser and his gold to shew how mere means to happiness may, from habit and association, be regarded as ends in themselves; or the comparison of the Deductive Method to ascending and descending a mountain only to reach the same level. A clear indication of the laborious care with which Mill constructed and composed his works is got by noticing the very admirable way in which he gradually descends from an abstract statement of a principle, through a sufficient elaboration of it, to a clinching illustration or an effective climax. The following passage, which is one of the happiest in the whole of Mill's works, will illustrate this careful art and the pleasing effect resulting from it:—

"The increasing specialisation of all employments; the division
"of mankind into innumerable small fractions, each engrossed by
"an extremely minute fragment of the business of society, is not
"without inconveniences, as well moral as intellectual, which, if
"they could not be remedied, would be a serious abatement from
"the benefits of advanced civilization. The interests of the
"whole—the bearings of things on the ends of the social union—
"are less and less present in the minds of men who have so con-
"tracted a sphere of activity. The insignificant detail which
"forms their whole occupation—the infinitely minute wheel they
"help to turn in the machinery of society—does not arouse or
"gratify any feeling of public spirit, or unity with their fellow
"men. Their work is a mere tribute to physical necessity, not
"the glad performance of a social office. This lowering effect of
"the extreme division of labour tells most of all on those who are
"set up as the lights and teachers of the rest. A man's mind is
"as fatally narrowed, and his feelings towards the great ends of
"humanity as miserably stunted, by giving all his thoughts to the

"classification of a few insects or the resolution of a few equations,
"as to sharpening the points or putting on the heads of pins."[1]

We must make brief mention also of Mill's terse, compressed, epigrammatic style. We are surprised at times with clinching brevity and unlooked-for smartness in antithesis and epigram. Though he is often ponderous, he is never verbose. He will not use two words where one will do. He is never quite fluent, and is exceedingly sparing and exact in his use of words. Though Mill neglected the artistic quality of prose he was sufficiently alive to those properties of style which are potent over men's minds to cause him to acquire certain effective modes which to some extent make up for his limitations of taste. He had a keen appreciation of French literature and admired the smartness of the French no less than their refinement. One of the qualities which his study of French writers led him to cultivate was epigram. It is strange that the writer whose prose is frequently heavy and dull should at intervals aim at terse, epigrammatic sentences. Mill often adopts a clinching style where elaborate logic is out of place; and there is occasionally an abruptness that borders on epigram. When criticising Comte's principle, the freedom of thought, as being of merely negative value, he aptly says,—

"Everyone is free to believe that two and two make ten, but
"the important thing is to know that they make four."[2]

We have noticed, broadly speaking, two styles in Mill's writings. It is because of these widely different manners that they have been popular with persons of very diverse tastes and acquirements. The mixture makes his works very readable. He soon wearies of his definitions, his formulæ, his swollen, technical paragraphs, and descends to the plain-spoken effective style. Now though Mill was so transparently honest and candid that we could never think him capable of deception, it is nevertheless true that when the reader is being delighted by this change and the writer is relaxing himself in this popular, free style, most of the elements which can have no legitimate admittance find their way unobserved into his philosophy. We have been struggling through a dry technical paragraph; all is apparently logical and exact, but not very palatable and not quite convincing. Instead of being bored with this abstract philosophical mode of expression we are gently transported into everyday, familiar surroundings. It is here that by a looseness in a word, or by the freedom of

---

[1] *Auguste Comte and Positivism*, p. 94.   [2] *Auguste Comte*, p. 77.

(supposed) equivalent modes of expression, or by the introduction of an unnoticed factor in a plausible illustration, the exactness goes, and we are now convinced of what before was unconvincing. What, for example, can appear more straightforward than the following popularly framed argument in Ch. iv. of the *Utilitarianism*; yet it is full of ambiguity and fallacy.

"The only proof capable of being given that an object is visible, is that people actually see it. The only proof that a sound is audible, is that people hear it; and so of the other sources of our experience. In like manner, I apprehend, the sole evidence it is possible to produce that anything is desirable, is that people do actually desire it."[1]

This is a mere play upon common words, and more fitting the mouth of a sophist or a word juggler than a candid enquirer. By an innocent loitering over such words as "visible" and "audible," used in the sense of that which *is* seen and heard, he artfully prepares the mind for accepting the commonplace word "desirable" as meaning that which is desired. If Mill were questioned from another standpoint, he would hold that "desirable" means what *ought* to be, and not what *is* desired. Mill's works contain many ambiguities and much looseness, due to the mixing of the accurate with the vague, the scientific and abstract with the popular and commonplace.

But we have not completed our review of Mill as a writer until his power as a polemist and dialectician has been remarked. He was well aware of his strength in this direction, and used it with very marked success. Powerful as a popular advocate, he is more so as a destructive and argumentative writer. Many men have damaged themselves and degraded their subject by betaking themselves to polemic; few have gained so much, by its means, as Mill. He was, perhaps, better equipped by natural endowments and by acquired qualities for this, than for any other kind of literary work. His keen logical gifts, his tact and practical common sense, his instinctive insight into the underlying motives and sentiments of an opponent, and his appreciation of the real strength of prejudice, made him a skilled tactician and a most politic antagonist. Moreover, the moral feelings which predominated in Mill's peculiarly-constituted emotional nature frequently operated most powerfully in his destructive style. There is indignation as well as powerful logic; moral intensity combined with calm, collected

[1] *Utilitarianism*, pp. 52, 53.

reserve. He manifests the keenest zest in argument, along with sincere love of truth and fair play. These nicely-balanced qualities make him a most formidable opponent, a severe critic, and a very powerful polemical writer. His modes of warfare are always honourable, and there is little in his argumentative or critical style that a candid opponent could object to. His sarcasm is sparing, and not at all ill-natured. His arguments are impersonal and his manner not violent, though his remarks are cutting. If he could avoid rousing prejudice he did so, not because of cowardice, but because the successful advocacy of opinions was dear to him. We never find him, from sheer pugnacity, running full tilt against opposition and prejudice. He takes the line of least resistance. His argumentative style is intrepid and unhesitating, yet he is never random, blustering, or offensively energetic. His blade is sharp, deft, and swift, but not brutal. He never loses control of himself, but is remarkably cool, even when most in earnest and most indignant. Mill's points are not gained by any very great subtlety, though there is skill in bringing an argument to bear on a vulnerable point and some ingenuity in dragging inconsistencies to light. There are frequent signs of the absence of metaphysical imagination, and the language is not flexible enough to follow the finest turns of meaning. But what is lost in subtlety and fine insight is gained in forceful dialectic. Mill's argumentative and critical styles are seen at their best in the destructive portions of his work entitled *The Examination of Sir William Hamilton's Philosophy*. Whatever our views as to the worth of Mill's strictures, these chapters excel as an elaborate critical handling of an opponent's doctrines. Perhaps Mill was never stirred so much as by Mansel's work, entitled the *Limits of Religious Thought*. He regarded its doctrines as so immoral as to permit himself to call it a "loathsome" book. When he attacks it in a digressive chapter of the *Examination*, his declamatory style rises to the highest point of passion and power we are aware it ever attained. We quote the passage, which contains a very famous climax :—

"If, instead of the 'glad tidings' that there exists a Being in
"whom all the excellences which the highest human mind can
"conceive, exist in a degree inconceivable to us, I am informed
"that the world is ruled by a being whose attributes are infinite,
"but what they are we cannot learn, nor what are the principles
"of his government, except that 'the highest human morality

"'which we are capable of conceiving' does not sanction them;
"convince me of it, and I will bear my fate as I may. But when
"I am told that I must believe this, and at the same time call this
"being by the names which express and affirm the highest human
"morality, I say in plain terms that I will not. Whatever power
"such a being may have over me, there is one thing which he
"shall not do: he shall not compel me to worship him. I will
"call no being good, who is not what I mean when I apply that
"epithet to my fellow-creatures; and if such a being can sentence
"me to hell for not so calling him, to hell I will go."[1]

Here, even along with impassioned force and amid the strongest modes of expression which Mill could summon to his aid, there is a calm dignity and nobility of bearing that is very remarkable in such a situation.

It remains for us to view, from the standpoint of literature, some of the more general features of our author's writings. Mill was not incapable of eloquence of a ponderous, oratorical kind, and we find that it is chiefly inspired by what may be called the master passion of his soul, human interest and sympathy. This is one of the few emotional forces that move his style. Mill's character was stamped with a high moral seriousness, and there is a pervading tone of melancholy. Not that his style is depressing; it is rather elevating and strengthening, for he had a stoic heart within him. But he is touched with the feeling of the misery of human life. This undercurrent of sadness is in keeping with his reserve of manner, while his stoic resignation well supported his calm dignity. It was this strong, permanent sympathy with humanity that was the real motive power of Mill the thinker and writer. It supplied the inspiration for persistent efforts to combine philosophic theory with genuine practical reforms in society and in thought. The highest pitch of fervour in his style is reached under the inspiration of this humanitarian sentiment.' At such points our author is very impressive though by no means overmastering. We quote below a passage in which Mill treats of the Religion of Humanity as advocated by Comte and adopted by himself. It is a period of great dignity and lofty eloquence:—

"The power which may be acquired over the mind by the idea
"of the general interest of the human race, both as a source of
"emotion and as a motive to conduct, many have perceived; but

---

[1] *Examination of Sir William Hamilton's Philosophy*, pp. 123, 124.

"we know not if anyone, before M. Comte, realised as fully as he
has done, all the majesty of which that idea is susceptible. It
ascends into the unknown recesses of the past, embraces the
manifold present, and descends into the indefinite and unfor-
seeable future. Forming a collective existence without assign-
able beginning or end, it appeals to that feeling of the Infinite,
which is deeply rooted in human nature, and which seems
necessary to the imposingness of all our highest conceptions. Of
the vast unrolling web of human life, the part best known to us
is irrevocably past; this we can no longer serve but still love:
it comprises for most of us the far greater number of those
who have loved us, or from whom we have received benefits, as
well as the long series of those who, by their labours and
sacrifices for mankind, have deserved to be held in everlasting
and grateful remembrance. As M. Comte truly says, the highest
minds, even now live in thought with the great dead, far more
than with the living; and, next to the dead, with those ideal
human beings yet to come, whom they are never destined to see.
If we honour as we ought those who have served mankind in the
past, we shall feel that we are also working for those benefactors
by serving that to which their lives were devoted. And when
reflection, guarded by history, has taught us the intimacy of the
connection of every age of humanity with every other, making
us see in the earthly destiny of mankind the playing out of a
great drama, or the action of a prolonged epic, all the generations
of mankind become indissolubly united in a single image,
combining all the power over the mind of the idea of Posterity,
with our best feelings towards the living world which surrounds
us, and towards the predecessors who have made us what
we are."[1]

Mill's art is rather of the rhetorical than of the literary type. It is not easy to read his prose without falling into an oratorical, declamatory swing and tone as the ear catches the sonorousness of the words and the weighty, measured sway of the sentences. In some of his later works, and especially in his political compositions, there is an impassioned oratory that contrasts strangely with the cold, abstract style of the scientific teacher. His general manner is characterised by plainness and solidity. The sentences are carefully constructed, but

---

[1] *Auguste Comte and Positivism*, p. 135.

merely with a view to utility. He writes as one would lay the foundations of an edifice, with regularity and strength, but without attempt at grace or adornment. His tastes and finer feeling were not sufficiently cultivated or drawn upon greatly to influence his writings, nor was his imagination strong enough to tinge them with any glow of more congenial light. The words he uses are conventional and plain; picturesque and highly-coloured forms of expression are vetoed. He has no love of words; that is, he has no pure love of speech. Speech is for him a medium merely, and its worth depends upon its adequacy and exactness, not its beauty or charm. Mill gained much by effective persuasion, nothing by artistic literary appliances.

But Mill not only neglected the artistic properties of his medium, he had an habitual curb on natural expression of feeling. Hence, his style is marked by rigidity, formalism, and reserve. There is the lack of rapid movement, warm enthusiasm, and spontaneous bursts of feeling. He speaks to us, as it were from a distance, *through* his medium not *in* it. The effect of this reserved manner on his writings is to give them a chilly, uncongenial atmosphere. It is this that produces so uncomfortable a feeling in many readers; a feeling experienced by Caroline Fox and well expressed in her *Memoirs*. She speaks of "that terrible book of John Mill's on Liberty, so clear "and calm and cold. . . . Mill makes me shiver, his blade is "so keen and unhesitating." It is difficult to explain this severe tone of Mill's writings in the face of the declarations of those who knew him that he was a man of unusual depth of feeling. This his style seems to belie; and the popular opinion of Mill is, that he was a cold, passionless, intellectual machine. This misrepresentation of the man by his own style is caused by that obstinate impenetrable reserve of manner for which his early training was largely responsible. He is far from being so vivid and realistic in his conceptions as our greatest philosophical writers. And he largely succeeds in stripping his thought and his expression of anything that would make it Mill's rather than anyone else's. Hence the fact that his feelings have so little effect on his general literary manner. His motives were mainly of the lofty, severe and moral type. However this may be, the marked impression we get from the study of our author is that he has not revealed his deepest nature in his style. Next to this reserve of manner, the tone that most uniformly pervades Mill's prose is a certain serene dignity well befitting deep thought and pure aims. He has not the lordly air of Bacon, and there is a total absence of gaudy, affected grandeur, but in its place there is a quiet unostentatious dignity that is very impressive. We ever have that sense of confidence which is produced by a style felt to be working well within its limits. There is no faltering weakness, neither is there nervousness or fuss. There is the carriage of one who has not the slightest misgiving as to the genuineness and importance of his own endeavour. Mill's was a lofty, dignified soul and his style never belies this character. The more we study his writings, the more we feel him to be, what Mr. Gladstone has called him,—the "Saint of Rationalism."

www.ingramcontent.com/pod-product-compliance
Lightning Source LLC
Chambersburg PA
CBHW021947160426
43195CB00011B/1253